**The Journey of Creating
Wealth & Happiness**

Written by
"Infitain" Sean Mitchell Caldwell

Dedicated to my daughter Wisdom
and all the people around the world that made this possible

CONTENTS

Aries – I Am

Often I found myself waking up in the middle of the night filled with creative thoughts, some of my best works may have come from those particular moments. At this time, I am not writing to sound like a scholar, or a great businessman, nor am I attempting to portray this great literary artist who won't have any grammatical errors, but a human who felt like he had something to share from his life experiences.

I've always felt the desire to write a book, I can recall being in the second grade and creating one about my life; of course this book didn't contain any serious life experiences, what could I have been writing about at that age other than the bike I didn't know how to ride, and things like the tv that sat in my kitchen apartment. Growing up I always thought it was cool to be able to say "Yeah, I wrote a book in the second grade." I threw it around a lot and didn't hesitate to include it now. Key moments like that shape and define who we grow to be. So with this I say, keep your eye on the youth and cultivate their talents…

What you are reading right now is a product of overwhelming thoughts, insomnia, sadness, confusion, somehow even loneliness; as my daughter and possible wife to be sleep in the other room. So much can be said about them alone, but I want to have tunnel vision on the point I am trying to make. You may be given missions in life that other people just won't be a part of. Before I committed to writing this book I felt as if I was almost going insane. I was literally shaking and full of ideas, so full of energy that the Universe was making me feel uncomfortable. At the time I didn't know what to make of that energy I shed a few tears thinking about the huge social responsibility I felt for mankind. I turned on the tv to search for inspiration, searching for someone to say to me what I would say to myself...

Approximately it is 1:38am and earlier yesterday at 3:30am I woke up from the sound of the cat "Miu Miu" snoring which actually woke me up again about an hour ago. As I awoke yesterday I got up and begin to write in a composition book I had been filling up for the past few years.

" I drew a blueprint "

I drew a blueprint for a piece of art I had been inspired to make about the culture of Hip Hop (Thank You J.R. Wheels of Soul West Philly R.I.P). The page on the left was blank and ripped in half but I wrote to be sold for $1,000,000 or best offer. I mean the nerve of me to even think that was possible right... I took a picture of it and put it on Instagram and labeled it "3am thoughts".

Being filled with so much excitement I decided to get ready for a two-hour drive to my hometown of Philadelphia to promote and sale an Autobiographical Hip Hop album I created titled *Timeless Masterpiece* and a short film I produced that comes with it.

As you may be able to decipher I had a lot going on in life, but if you were to ask my girlfriend she may have said I was lazy and sat on the couch all day staring at my computer, as I am doing so right now but perspective is everything. She was actually pissed off that I would leave the house at 4:30am to go sale my cd. The sun didn't even rise yet, but that was the point of me doing it. I wanted to clock in before the sun did (Sounds cool doesn't it). In life there will be people that will have no idea why you do the things that get placed in your spirit, sometimes you won't know fully yourself either. But the same little voice that spoke to me to write the book in the second grade that was only 10 -15 pages was the same little voice that spoke to me to get up and race the sun to shine in Philly. My girlfriend said nobody is going to buy something from you in the dark that early, but to the contrary, I was able to make my first sale at approximately 6:31am before the sun was due to rise at 7:19am. It felt rewarding not just to prove her wrong and document it eternally in this book, but it felt rewarding to be outside in 25 degrees bright and early seeing the people up with holiday coffee cups about to start their work day the same as I was. It felt rewarding to be the early bird that got the worm.

Perhaps if I didn't obey that voice that told me to get up and go, you would not be reading this at the moment.

" He was only identifying the negatives in his life "

I met an interesting person that morning I can't remember his name, but his face is clear as day in my mind. He was a Caucasian guy with a freshly shaved face, he was bundled up and carrying bags but it was cold as bizzaro hell outside so who wasn't bundled up. As he walked by I told him that he had the light of God in his eyes. I tend to say things like that to people if I notice a particular look in their demeanor. He said, "I read him completely wrong" as he stopped to talk with me. I had a mission of my own, but I also take time to share kind words with people even if they don't buy anything from me. He said before I even try to sell him something that he was homeless. If you were to put a suit on this guy he looked like he could walk into any place and get hired, he had that *All-American* square jaw, presented a firm handshake, spoke intelligently but something within had to be holding him back. Perhaps his own vices with drugs, alcohol, or a life of dishonesty. We didn't get in to the particulars of his struggles but it's something I noticed he was definitely doing wrong that was keeping him down, he kept talking negatively about himself. The whole time we were talking he was only identifying the negatives in his life and his struggles with insecurity it sounded to me like he was not only his biggest critic but his worst enemy as well. I pointed it out to him that he was only saying negative things about himself and he said that people had been telling him that his whole life.

We spoke for about 15 minutes and I bring him up to identify a power in life that we all have. The power of how we speak, it's been identified by many people before me,

" The power of how we speak "

I know of this power because I have read it, and heard others speak about it. You may have heard successful people talk about it through their own experiences. It's been identified as *The Secret*, the power of thought. The Bible says we speak life and death out the power of the tongue. Some people will say the glass is half empty some will say it is half full. I'm sure you have heard some of these expressions before, but they will always be reassuring to the soul. I simply say to you at this moment speak the journey you wish to travel into existence

Over the years through doing my sales and marketing I found that the people I would try to stop in a crowd regardless of their race or gender shared a common look in their eye. I find it easy to equate the look with God because it is so broad, but if I had to define it more thoroughly I would say a person with vision, a person of strength, confidence, perhaps even love, a love for humanity, I found that these people create, or work with children, or connect with the spirit realm in some shape or form. This look transcends religion for I have witnessed people with the form of godliness but denying the power thereof. At times I have seen preachers with white collars wrapped around their neck, or a monk walking down the street wearing a robe and holding prayer beads and they did not possess this look at the moment I saw them. Although it is impossible to judge anyone and summarize their entire character off first glance.

" I have sold things to people literally all over the world "

While marketing my projects over the years I changed various techniques of how I would approach a potential customer to make a purchase. When I was younger I would walk up to any and everyone and put my cd directly in their hand and sell it, I made a lot of sales with that technique. I've always had the gift of gab "as they say" and the ability to articulate exactly what I wanted to convey. I found that communication was one of my biggest assets. I have sold things to people literally all over the world and was able to connect in just a few seconds. I was making $5 to $20 sales in less than one minute and moving on to the next person expeditiously.

Often, I would go back to the drawing board

As I matured I started introducing more props such as posters and cameras standing on tripods. I even used Virtual Reality glasses to preview some of my work, it was really a sight to behold. Often, I would go back to the drawing board thinking to myself how I can make it easier for people to stop and interact. I say this to speak on a very important question I developed in my sales pitch and it can be a major blessing to you if you apply it. The question is "**What do you do?**"

4 simple words can make a huge difference in your life or perhaps for someone else close to you. Imagine the answers I got when I started asking random people that question. For years I found myself standing on the corner of Broad and Chestnut in Philadelphia; right across the street from City Hall. It's people I would see for years and when I finally started to ask, " What do you do? ", that's when I discovered that these people were judges and City Council people, High powered attorneys, all kinds of stuff! Now how you utilize that information is within the mind of the beholder. How about I take the time to ask that question to you, it will be fun. Of course I won't hear the answer, but I pose the question to you.

What do you do?...

What came to mind, did you say your day job, does what you do for a living define you? It's a good exercise for younger people too, I would hear them say I am a student, or I am a waiter, or perhaps a person would say I don't do anything… We must be able to speak what we want out of our life into existence. If you are an artist that's working at a job to pay the bills don't define yourself as the employee. Speak to the world that I am an Artist, I create! You would be surprised what opportunities come your way if you spoke about your talents and skills. Be sure to define yourself and not let your strawman do it for you (that's a whole different book that you have to get from someone else I'm not going too deep into that).

The homeless guy I spoke of earlier did not speak his opportunities into existence, he even labeled himself as homeless which I could only describe him as.

Another Bible reference I will use is let those that are poor say I am rich, let those that are sick say I am well. It's not about being naive to real life, but it's about taking command of your thoughts which is one of the only real things we can take control of. I am an Artist, a Successful Business Man, I am a visionary, a producer, a director, a writer, I create and Manifest my thoughts into reality.

" Only those who dare will see it appear "

I've been trying to think of this really cool saying and it finally came to me. Only those who dare will see it appear. What does that sound like to you?

Every person has different reasons for reading this, my mission was to write it and share it with as many people as I could. If you are anything like me and that's the person I believe I am speaking to right now, you are feeling motivated you are feeling strong, ready to tackle the world and whatever challenges come your way. I find that it's good to digest something if it really has meaning.

I would suggest right now you take the time to write a to do list, things that are obtainable. Things that can be accomplished within a year's time nothing beyond that. It's good to have a 5-year plan but the journey of 1,000 miles begins with a single step. Set some goals and start marking them off as you achieve them. Keep a journal of your ideas and the things you want to manifest if you don't already have one. Take notes of the jewels you get from what you are reading, keep in mind that I am sharing things that I have heard other places as well as things I have done that made a huge difference in my own journey.

I've had a composition book that I had for about 2 years and I wrote about 20 goals, from getting my driver's license, to a passport, a professional high-end camera, to completing my album I was inspired to do. If I look at it now, all of those things are marked off, so what does that mean? It's time to start another list. I didn't have a definitive plan of what I wanted this book to be about I know I wanted to share my thoughts, and experiences.

" We all have the potential to be whatever it is we can envision "

Like I said earlier I am not going to pretend to be something I am not. (At this very moment) I am not a Millionaire in the physical but in all actuality, I know spiritually I am wealthy. As you read I welcome you to a look into my life's journey over the next year. Look at me like a friend that's sharing his experiences along the way, I feel like the more human you know I am the more you can know that you can unlock the greatness in your own life I say these things not as an egomaniac but as a man that KNEW he was on the verge of figuring it out himself. It is all connected one *Timeless Masterpiece*, you, me, my daughter and wife to be, sleeping in the other room, and the loved ones you have in your life, even the homeless man who didn't profess his own greatness.

We all have the potential to be whatever it is we can envision ourselves to be. Nobody sets the limit but you.

Where can you see yourself? What do you deserve? In time those things may change as you mature into YOU, and not what you do to keep up with society. I have not had the pleasure yet to speak in a room of over 1000 people. But I can see it. I see people taking notes, I see people smiling and laughing, I was going to be facetious and say I saw someone dozing off, but you know what, I don't see that. I see the greatness and potential in all their eyes. I see you...

" I felt the potential to be great my whole life, I just didn't know what medium it would be "

At this very moment there is about $14. in my bank account. Keep in mind I have been self-employed for over 10 years and have been discovering who I am every day. I felt the potential to be great my whole life, I just didn't know what medium it would be.

" The only way you're going to the NBA is if you buy a ticket "

I once thought I would play basketball in the NBA, there was a basketball court in my neighbor's Mr. Sonny backyard next door to me growing up. I had a good friend by the name of Onaje that I played ball with almost every day for years. Once upon a time I said to my cousin Hope "I'm going to the NBA", he said to me and I quote. " The only way you're going to the NBA is if you buy a ticket " (take time to laugh at that) I was a HORRIBLE basketball player so bad I capitalized each letter in the word horrible, I'm about 5'8 no amazing dribbling or passing skills. I miss about 90% of the shots I put up, I can't dunk I completely suck if you will…

" What I did have right was the heart of a champion, the spirit of an MVP "

I didn't necessarily need him to tell me that but I can appreciate his honesty. What I did have right was the heart of a champion, the spirit of an MVP, someone that would give 100% to himself, his teammates, and the people who cheered him on along the way. Till this day I still equate a lot of scenarios in life to basketball. Perhaps I will make those comparisons throughout this book. The fact you are reading this book shows how much I was in the gym (figuratively).

There had to be a mental commitment to write this as I speak to you in the huddle. We are going to win this game called life, I'm rooting for you like I'm rooting for myself. I had to discover the paths I was called to be great in. Yes, we all have a choice in life but I don't mind contradicting myself and speaking on destiny. I was destined to write this the same way you were destined to read it. I shared that I had $14 dollars in my bank account so you could see how much we had in common for richer or for poorer. I hope you have much more than that to your name because a good financial cushion is always great to have.

As I get ready to enter the new year I do not owe anyone any money all of my bills are caught up, I have High Quality professional cameras and equipment, Thousands of business cards, multiple websites, a passport to travel anywhere in the world when need be, a driver's license and car to get around with and a few hundred bucks cash which I am planning to spend most of on my family for the holidays. But most importantly I have gratitude for my health, for they say health is wealth, and I pray my mind stays clear to manifest as you see the words in motion. I share all this to say. I have invested so much time and money and gained so much experience that I am going into the new year prepared to win. It's the start of a new season as we suit up to win this championship together. I'm ready and I hope you are too, if you need to sit on the bench by all means sit back read and watch and peep game. I want the ball, but I am ready to pass it when my teammates are open. I'm ready to play defense and hustle up and down the court. We are going to play smart not just aggressive, The Most High is the coach and has put us together to Win this Championship. There is no competition just a challenge for us to accomplish.

I

Capricorn - I Use

Today I heard news from my Aunt Jean that my father failed his drug test and had to severe 60 days in a halfway house. Now my Dad just came home from prison doing 28 years. I was about 3 years old when he went. Believe it or not I don't hold any ill will towards him I guess maybe because my Mother didn't speak negatively about him as I grew up. Since my father was released a little over a year ago it didn't take him long to get back into the streets. But I must say it was a pleasure to get to see and spend time with him. One thing my father did was keep in touch with me the best way we could. I grew up looking forward to his letters often several pages, the longer the letter the better I recall. I have very early memories of my mother reading me his words, but my whole life my father came in the form of a letter. He always addressed me as Mr. Sean Mitchell Caldwell on the envelope. In my heart all I can do is appreciate him being there even in that manner. I can't go as far as saying he was a good man, he actually was somewhat proud to admit he was a criminal, but he was a good father to some degree. He never missed a Birthday without sending a card he even did some wrong things from time to time and sent me money and sneakers somehow some way. In a world where unfortunately fathers are not around for their children I was grateful to have a connection with him even if it was from a distance. The news of him getting into trouble again didn't strike me hard but with my own self-inflicted pressure to strive for greatness perhaps I felt a small form of resentment.

" I am taking the pain of what I may be feeling and I am seeing the silver lining through the experience "

As you read this at this very moment I am taking the emotions of what is really a bad situation and have provided thee with lemonade. Do you see what I am doing? I am taking the pain of what I may be feeling and I am seeing the silver lining through the experience and I'm sharing it with you. How much cooler does it make what you are reading with an opening chapter like this. This is 100% my life and if I really began to share more about what is going on this would be more of a diary than I would want it to be. See I want us to look at this together, I'm not going to stay focused on the problems and say woe is me throughout this entire book. I challenge you to do the same whatever is going on in your life. I don't know if I would still be here if I only looked at my problems. Let me tell you a little about myself so you can get a better understanding of why I feel I have the audacity to write to you this way.

At the end of the day I'm a Momma's Boy,

I was raised in a little duplex where my home was on the second floor above a beauty salon. My early years

I grew up with my Mother Linda, my brother Terrell and my Aunt Carolyn. My Aunt had our living room as her room and I shared a room with my brother who is 7 years older than me. Most of the time I wanted to sleep in my mother's room until I was around 8 or 9 maybe even older to make it sound a little better. My Mother was my best friend growing up and I talked to her freely just as she was.

" Sadly, when I was in the eleventh grade I lost my Mother to cancer which was devastating "

It was just my brother and I in the house at the time of my Mom's passing. My brother was a workaholic and always kept a good-looking girlfriend so after a while I didn't see him that much at home. I started to really raise myself as I started working 40 to 50 hours a week while still going to school. School started seeming more of a social gathering than me taking the institution seriously, I mean I was dealing with the death of the closest person to me. I was still a Momma's boy so I had to adjust to life.

" We have to be able to use the things that challenge us and allow it to fuel us on the journey ahead "

In life they say you have to roll with the punches and that is very much true. They also say that the only thing in life that is certain is death and having to deal with that so early matured me and kept me immature at the same time if that makes any sense. We must be able to use the things that challenge us and allow it to fuel us on the journey ahead. I'm sure at some time you had to deal with the death of losing a loved one and yes it hurts and even until this day I may randomly out of nowhere shed tears thinking of her. I miss her, but life is life and we are all due to expire within our physical shell at some point in time. Keeping that in mind we must not hesitate to tell and show our loved ones how much we care about them. If you really love someone we can't take our time with them for granted. Love is an action word, it has to be expressed, felt, so I request if you are in position get up and hug one of your loved ones if they are close by. Look up and smile at a stranger and say hello. Call a friend or family member you haven't *spoken* to in a little while. Don't ask for anything just reach out and show the love, it goes a long way…

Those dots represented the pause break for you to really do it.

The Domino Effect

Today's forecast called for rain in the A.M until midafternoon. I had spent all but $60 of every dollar I had to my name to do some Christmas shopping for my family. I've been working outside promoting and marketing my business for about 12 years now. I used to do Telemarketing which I was pretty good at then one day I decided to quit and take my record label INFITAINMENT more seriously and sell records independently. People like Puff Daddy and Master P were my biggest influences to do so.

" I invested a little over a thousand dollars and this was the birth of INFITAINMENT "

I had a close friend named Brandon who had asked me to help him put together a cd for him for a music conference which was easy for me to do. Prior to that while in high school I had two friends by the name of Shawn and Alan who put together a cd themselves and let people hear it in school. They called it A&A which stood for Authentic and Al, Authentic was Shawn's rap name. When they made that cd that was the inspiration to say I'm going to start a record label and call it Infinite Entertainment which later became INFITAINMENT.

One of my biggest contributions was I had a video camera; this was before smartphones, so I was collecting footage of all kinds of things back then. To add onto my so-called record label at the time I went to a company called Disc Makers and ordered a cd duplicator, 1000 blank cds and cases, as well as a cd printer and a Micron Computer that I had built for about $300. I invested a little over a thousand dollars and this was the birth of INFITAINMENT.

" I kept investing "

One day Young Al who now called himself Bobby Drake was at my house and we recorded a whole bunch of music on a digital recorder, we decided to make a cd out of it and named it the Prologue. The sound quality was horrible but at the time I was so motivated and inspired I pressed up hundreds of copies. Having no clear direction and a few bucks, I kept investing. I went to a local producer named Problemz who a friend of mine named Rafiq connected me with. I asked Problemz how much for production and studio time for a song I had in mind for Bobby Drake to record. He charged me $400. for it which if I had better connections I could have got a complete professional album recorded but I believed what I was doing was right and I was willing to invest my time and money.

" Sometimes the energy you put into to your vision is about learning "

Thinking back, I never had a plan what was going to bring success, but I was doing something right from day one. I was taking initiative and investing. Sometimes the energy you put into to your vision is about learning and as the old saying goes experience is the best teacher. You must be willing to take losses to win, some people may look at it as if I was wasting money but as I look back, it all was worth it.

" Some call it a Spirit Guide, some call it God, some call it Intuition "

I decided to leave my hometown of Philly and go to Ohio to stay with my brother John and his family, John was actually the first person to buy a cd from me. My friend Brandon "B" thought it was a horrible idea but I felt like it was the right thing to do especially while trying to find myself after losing my mother not long before.

In life I have learned that some things don't have to make sense to anyone, not even yourself at times. You should trust that still voice inside of you, some call it a Spirit Guide, some call it God, some call it intuition, perhaps it's just our own thoughts and freewill. I needed to be around more family, so I am grateful for the choice I made.

I took those few hundred copies of the Prologue with the intentions to sell them as Master P had did Independently. I had the gift of gab and even growing up I was selling things and making deals, I was a natural. I remember going to a mall in Ohio where my niece Natia worked and taking about 10 cds and a cd player. I was by myself and damn near petrified in all actuality I am introverted and can even be considered shy at times, lots of people would find that hard to believe but I naturally can be a reserved person, a lone wolf even. I conjured up the courage to stop someone, I played them the music and they couldn't get past the bad sound quality. I had received my first no. At the time I didn't realize how great that no was for my business but from doing telemarketing that had prepared me to know that comes with the territory with business. I had asked a few more people and kept hearing no. Finally, I stopped an older woman and it happened, my first yes. I sold the Prologue for $10. My first dollar earned for my business INFITAINMENT, but I didn't cherish the moment as I do now, I wish I knew what it would become I would have kept that ten-dollar bill for memorabilia.

" the world wasn't going to give me anything just because I showed up "

I stuck it out for another hour and guess how many more I sold? Nothing, nada, zilch, I felt defeated somehow in my mind I thought all I had to do was create anything, put my name on it and the rich fairy was going to wave its wand and I was going to be some type of overnight success. I was in Ohio for an entire summer and with hundreds of cds I sold a total of 3, one to my brother, one to that lady, and one more to a couple that gave me $5. which was half of what I was selling the Prologue for. It was a real wake up call for my young ambition, the world wasn't going to give me anything just because I showed up, and guess what, the world isn't going to give you anything either.

My ego was crushed I was still the same kid that thought he was going to the NBA with no skills… I slipped into some form of depression/ I became very lazy and afraid to interact socially. I decided it was time to go back to Philadelphia, my brother Terrell was maintaining the apartment we grew up in so luckily I was welcomed back. I brought that depression back to Philly with me. I had changed I left young and ambitious and returned with no money, and a weight of disappointment.

Before I continue I pose a question, who determined how many cds I was going to sell in Ohio? Was it the dozen people that said no, or was it me? I think you know the answer to that… But destiny is destiny perhaps if I would have found success selling my cds in Ohio I may have never returned to Philly to become the person I am today. I had more family there then I did in Philly so that was a serious possibility. My Brothers John, Nate, Michael and my sister Donna who are all my Fathers children had migrated with their Mom Margaret to stay there for good.

My brother Terrell in Philly was still working all the time so most of the time it was me about 20 years old with no job. I didn't bring food into the house and my brother ate out most of the time and had a girlfriend so there was not much food in the house. Normally on the weekend I would go to my Aunt Carolyn and my little cousin Brianne house to eat dinner, so I wasn't completely out of luck. Often I went to B's house and could sleep and get a good meal from his Mom Miss Debbie. She was always inviting and let me come there anytime and I love and appreciate her until this day.

" You would have definitely considered me to be a loser at this time "

Hanging out with Brandon who we can refer to as B for now on I got more into Cannabis. He was the Snoop Dogg of West Philly and you know birds of a feather flock together. Marijuana wasn't a thing in my house growing up but it was always there at B's. Now I was grown and you can never blame anyone for your mistakes, but the abuse of anything can be harmful. If you eat McDonalds everyday you will see a significant change in your health. Mary Jane became my thing, my apartment, at B's house, with Authentic, it was my way to be social. But with that came many bad choices as well. I was not in a clear frame of mind. Some people can engage in Marijuana or alcohol and get up and go to work the next day and be on time and maintain but I was young and irresponsible, my brother was so into his own life he couldn't really see how much it was affecting me.

To get money I was breaking into his room and stealing his change he collected just to get by and eat

Chinese food. I was a complete wreck. My weight was down, I never got professional haircuts, you would have definitely considered me to be a loser at this time.

" I idolized Puff Daddy growing up, that was a true inspiration to why I wanted to be in the Music Business. "

Prior to that when I was working I use to go shopping and buy clothes and keep myself fresh. My addiction then was Sean John, all throughout High School that's what I would wear. I idolized Puff Daddy growing up, that was a true inspiration to why I wanted to be in the Music Business. That era of Hip Hop, with Biggie, 2pac, and the so-called East coast West coast beef was my generation. I was drawn to it, perhaps it was fate. Puff Daddy name was Sean C. for Combs, my name was Sean C. for Caldwell. He was a Scorpio, I am a Scorpio, his Dad was a Hustler, my Dad was a Hustler, I was a fan. In total just because my name was Sean and his clothing line was Sean John, I spent thousands on the clothes over the years. One day something hit me to give it all away.

See I had engulfed myself so much into that my friend Pooh would even call me Diddy. I went to school with Pooh and was cool with him because he lived on B's block on 56 street in West Philly. Pooh was actually the first-person B hit the ganja with but Pooh was able to not let it take over his life, so he wasn't really into it. Back in the day, it was always Me, Pooh, and a good friend of mine named Jawsh. Pooh and I even worked together at a nursing home. I even began to call his Mom Aunt. But once I got heavy into the trees our friendship started to drift apart. They were not those kinds of people and you can see the change in me. I was different,

" One thing that didn't change was my idea for INFITAINMENT "

I had got this jacket airbrushed so even when I wasn't doing anything with the business I was promoting which was highly effective.

To get away from the Autobiography feel for a second and back to where I am today mentally. You have to completely submerge yourself in your vision. Even when I wasn't really doing anything with INFITAINMENT that was making money, I had created an identity with it. People knew that I had a record label. That I was in the entertainment business because I wore it on my back, literally. Looking back that was the best thing I had going on. Walking through the hood, on the bus, or in the Chinese store I had on my jacket and people knew I was about that life.

We as artist, or business people have to let it be known. You must speak it into existence. I was that guy with the Infinite entertainment airbrushed jacket. What did I do, absolutely nothing, I didn't rap, I didn't produce really, hell I didn't even know what my contribution was going to be to the Industry but if anything, I was the guy that had the airbrushed jacket on, so you knew I was about something.

" Sometimes the best thing we can do for a person with problems is not enable them "

Still not working and breaking into Brothers room every other day he just got fed up. He said I was acting like a crackhead he knew I was taking his change and felt like it was time to move on with his life. I was not the innocent Momma's boy I once was and can understand his decision. He didn't know it at the time or maybe he did but that tough love in the long run made me a better person. Sometimes the best thing we can do for a person with problems is not enable them. Love is Love but if a person is not loving themselves and making good decisions you end up getting walked on and taken advantage of. I didn't grow because it was too easy for me to smoke weed and not face my problems. I was content with being a high school dropout with no job, no income, and was living in a fantasy of being a record label exec.

With my brother preparing to leave and with no income I had to find a job immediately. B's older Brother Shawn was a manager at a Vitamin store and was able to hook me up with a job. It was perfect timing because my brother Terrell was serious and left for Chicago. I had no way to pay the rent which wasn't that expensive, but it had to be paid. I worked at that Vitamin store and learned the ins and outs of it. I became good at selling vitamins and doing my job. I got the bills turned into my name and was doing ok maintaining everything for a little while on my own. 20 years old, my own place, a little bit of money I wasn't doing too bad. I had my living room set up as my home office. I still had all my equipment and could make cds very easily. Before my brother left he gave me an editing software for my computer which allowed me to control wav files better. I could now record more professionally from just using a digital recorder. My Brother Terrell and I don't communicate as much as I would like to, but that gift was a great asset to me and helped mold my arrangement skills and do lots of future projects.

Almost a year passed as I was working getting by paying bills, the store manager (who oddly resembled Stone-Cold Steve Austin) one day pulled me to the side and in a nice way told me I was fired. FIRED... what was I supposed to do now, I was maintaining my apartment keeping up with bills and everything. I remember the feeling of wanting to knock all the vitamins off the shelves as I left but what good would that have done. If I was more mature perhaps I would've immediately searched for a new job, but I slowly slipped back into a little depression. Keep in mind I was in my early 20's no high school diploma with no real guidance or authority figure to give me advice. I was still living in the house I grew up in. I never left home, life kind of forced me into the situation.

Within that time, I remember slowly getting behind in my rent.

Being that my Mother, and even Grandmother had rented from the landlord Mr. George for so many years I think they were a little lenient with me. I remember getting my first girlfriend Iesha to move in with me and help with the bills. We were not romantically involved but a part of me was thinking we would somehow end up happily ever after, Iesha was my first love in high school and the only girl my Mother ever really met who I dated. She became a friend of the family, so it didn't seem too much like a bad idea.

I can go into all the reasons why it didn't work out but just to expedite the trip down memory lane I was able to land a job doing telephone surveys which I was really good at. I was a natural phone person and a good talker. I would switch between doing day shift and night shift over the course of time I was there. Being that Iesha name wasn't on the lease she had to leave on not the best of terms. But I appreciate her timing and being there when I needed her, she is still a friend of the family until this day in my eyes. My Mom really liked her so on that note alone our friendship is frozen in time.

" Submerging yourself in your art, business or whatever vision you've been given is the best way to bring it to fruition "

I was once again on my own working to maintain the good foundation I had been given growing up. I worked there for a few years but while I was there I was investing more into INFITAINMENT, I had upgraded my jacket that looked even more legit, this version was embroidered and said INFITAINMENT "More Than Just A Label" on the back. It was black with metallic silver stitching and had red sleeves. I took much pride in wearing it and made me look more serious.

Once again as an artist or business person that's what we have to do, it wasn't much but even that jacket made a huge impact on my journey in life. I found that submerging yourself in your art, business or whatever vision you've been given is the best way to bring it to fruition. You have to bring it to life in some shape or form. If you have such a vision that isn't fully up and running I highly suggest creating yourself a poster, a button, getting some business cards and claiming who you want to be.

With the combination of having the jacket and a few people in the hood seeing that I was able to create quality looking cds. INFITAINMENT existed. I recall being at B's house one day and his good friend Shizz came in listening to a cd by a guy I went to middle school with named Craig. He went by the name Nitty Rosco, Shizz was so in to the music that it was inspiring, it was one of the first times I saw someone listening to music by someone I knew personally and genuinely liking it. I remember reaching out to Craig a few months later to see if we could work on something. I invited him to the home office and we put together a project called *The Best of Nitty 2*, I took the picture for the cover and compiled about 15 songs he recorded and put them on cd using the software my brother had got for me. I made sure I expanded the brand by putting INFITAINMENT on the cover. I think I gave him about 50 copies of the cds and that was pretty much that.

Live 8

Around this time there was a huge concert by the name of *Live 8* where thousands of people had gathered to watch at the Philadelphia Parkway. The concert had various bands performing there and artist of different genres having something for everybody. Going to Live 8 literally changed my life by seeing all those different types of people come together for a common cause, it was truly inspiring.

What I'm about to share was life changing and really set me on the path that I am on today. I'm not sure if it was the telemarketing and the phone surveys I was doing at my day job, but I got the idea to create a petition and set a goal to get 1000 signatures to do an event in my neighborhood in West Philly. I titled it T.R.Y *Teaching Reality to Youth.* With INFITAINMENT as the organization putting it together one day I went out on the journey alone to get those signatures. Keep in mind in my personal life I am not the most outgoing person I prefer to be reserved and not noticed. If I go to a restaurant I don't like to speak loudly or anything like that, but when I challenged myself to get those 1,000 signatures, all those things were out the window.

" I was completely dedicated "

I was walking into barber shops introducing myself and getting signatures along with phone numbers and emails. While people were waiting for the bus I would introduce myself and tell them about the vision and get them to sign. I was completely dedicated to seeing the spreadsheet I had created on *Microsoft Excel* filled up until I reached 1,000 signatures. I was introducing myself to neighbors I had lived around my whole life and never had a chance to get to know them. It was something spiritually humane about getting those signatures.

EBR

One of the best things I got from the experience was the words of wisdom I received along the way. The universe was maturing me through my interaction with complete strangers. Lots of people stood out to me but one person in particular by the name of Earl Byron Russell "EBR" said three words to me that I would take and to gross over a quarter million dollars while being self-employed. "Master E" I grew to call him was a former Martial Arts instructor in West Philadelphia. I first met him walking down the street collecting signatures around an area of 60th and Haverford. He was sitting on his porch as I approached telling him about my mission. He was quick to sign my petition then shared a little about himself, now here was a tall guy, not overweight but big with a few missing teeth. He was intimidating by nature but kind and knowledgeable. He told me to condition my body to drop down and slowly do 10 pushups any time I thought about it, funny I just did 10 pushups before I started writing this evening which happens to be New Year's Eve. It's 11:00pm at this very moment so I guess I'll say happy new year to you just to save this moment in time. I guess I dragged out the 3 words he shared long enough, I just wanted to set it up to prolong the power of the words. I hope these 3 words fuel you as much as they did me over the years. He told me "Persistence beats Resistance" I mean just 3 words, but boy did they have an impact on my life. I'm not sure where he heard the slogan, but it was brought to me by EBR who will be forever immortalized in this book as well as his past accomplishments. He planted those seeds in my mind and spirit and they continue to grow and bear fruit to this day.

" There is no trying "

I remember another elder by the name of Ubaid, who shared some great words of Wisdom that I keep with me until this day. He told me "there is no trying" we either do it or we don't.. I tend not to use the word try nowadays. I didn't try to write a book, you are reading it right now, it is done. Trying leaves room for things not to be completed. There were lots of other things I heard along the way while collecting those signatures and lots of great people as well. I highly recommend the challenge of doing something along those lines of collecting signatures for any reason. I found it builds character and is a great way to network and meet new people. Perhaps perform a survey testing out your idea or anything that causes you to interact with people outside of your normal circle.

" I obtained a permit "

After I got those 1,000 signatures I obtained a permit to host the event at a neighborhood park named Carol park in my community (Thank you Brotha Ubaid). I didn't need those signatures to obtain the permit, but it felt good to do it. It was truly the journey and not the destination. I envisioned the event to be so much more than what took place, but I was young, and one person. That was when I was first introduced to the world of nonprofit status 501c3. Keep in mind I didn't have any serious money to rent a stage and a sound system or Porta

Potties and stuff like that, but you would be surprised what things are obtainable with the proper information. I heard another cool saying years later that I keep with in my rolodex of inspiration. "Prior Planning Prevents Poor Performance" I look forward to putting together another event in the future, and when I do it again, it will be done correctly. As I said before, and I'm sure you have heard it as well, experience is the best teacher. I remember the faces of a few people who showed up to the park that day disappointed and expected more as I did.

(HAPPY NEW YEAR)

Currently as I write it's a few days after the new year and I'm excited to finish up looking at the past. I wanted you as a reader to get to know me a little better and understand how I got to the point where I am now. A very interesting thing occurred Christmas eve as I was out doing my Sales and Marketing in front of Madison Square Garden. It was later in the day and I met a guy who was a little intrigued by my presentation, he was challenging me as a salesman to see how good I really was, he even stated that I probably wasn't good enough to get him to buy something from me. I love challenging moments like that and I feel it brings out the best in me. (Embrace Challenges). He stuck around a little bit and watched me draw people in and was impressed by my technique. What is that technique you ask? It's a point of eye contact combined with a conscious look at a person's body language and subtitle hand motions to draw them in. I think that was a pretty good and accurate description on my behalf if I say so myself.

I asked the gentleman standing with me the Golden Question "What do you do?" He told me he hired people to work on Wall Street and was looking for 3 new people. He also stated I would be a great candidate for the position, I took it as the universe providing an escape for me if I was ready to throw in the entrepreneurial towel. Believe it or not YOU are one of the main reasons why I have decided to turn down the position. I told my little cousin Brianne who recently started college and of course she told me to take the job, I shared the news on social media and got a whole bunch of likes as people were encouraging me to take the job. Financially I know that would solve a lot of my problems but there is a burning desire within me to continue to build on this independent journey and sure the book may have sounded great saying I did all this to end getting a job on Wall Street. That would sound great for someone else's book, BUT NOT THIS ONE.

" Upon faith and work ethic "

This is a story about being dedicated to what you believe in and not giving up when things get tough. This is a story about one creating their own path in this world and truly building something upon faith and work ethic. There is a deep non-selfish factor within me that wants people like yourself to know it's possible. Lots of times we hear from people who have become successful and decided to share their story. I share this with you from a perspective in the midst thereof. Success is a state of mind and though my bank account does not scream that I am rich at the present moment, my biggest asset is faith. It's as if the universe made a promise that is confirmed within my heart and the ambition to watch it come to fruition.

" life is about balance "

As I write this at 1:54am challenges come my way to stop me from doing so. Sometimes in life the people closest to us will demand our time. There will be times your dreams and aspirations may seem like they are in competition with your personal life. I may have stated this before but even I must be reminded that life is about balance and one must be able to cherish what he has. Anything worth cherishing should be appreciated and held on to.

Life gradually started to change for me once I received those 1000 signatures. In fact now that I think of it, 1,000 has always been a key number for me. Earlier I spoke of ordering 1,000 blank cds and 1,000 cases for *The Prologue* project. I only pressed up a few hundred of them and had lots of blank disc left.

Music Over Business

My good friend B invested and went to a Philadelphia Music conference and wanted to take some of his recordings packaged up to give out. I helped him arrange a demo cd of some his best songs that he had available. Since around the age of fourteen he was in a rap group with some of his friends named Swat *Team* but decided to work on more solo works as time progressed. I think the demo was for a project he was doing called *To B or not to B*. He went to the conference with the cds and got a little motivated from doing so. All of this is significant history on how I became the person I am today.

The root of my business INFITAINMENT was assisting others and I spent many years doing so as we still do until this day. B and I have always taken time to communicate over the years and work on creative projects in many spectrums but found the most success in the music business. One day while at my home office we put together an entire cd called M.O.B: *Music Over Business"* *there* is someone who may be reading this who may say to themselves "I remember that".

Once we launched that CD it went on to be the core foundation of INFITAINMENT. We scanned a picture of a 5 dollar bill took some samples from the movie *What's Love Got To Do With It;* mainly because my cousin Hotep liked it so much that it rubbed off on me. We took about 10 to 15 songs B had did and put his artist name *B. Logic* on the cover. Being a young boss in his own right he wanted to have his own company which is respectable, B. Logic named his production company *Sleepless Knights Enterprises* which as of this day has been formed into an LLC. (Limited Liability Company) which he deserves a salute for. We titled Music over Business a Sleepless Knights/ INFITAINMENT production.

" We pressed up 25 cds "

Since the age of 6 years old we always had that business frame of mind. Just for the sake of nostalgia the first company we thought of was named S&B. Funny thinking back at 6 years old we were having business ideas for all kinds of things.

We pressed up 25 cds with no real idea of what to do with them. One Sunday we were both off from work I believe he was working at McDonalds at the time. I remember sitting with him in the back room of his Mother's house surrounded by records, his MPC beat machine, and his synthesizer keyboard that he saved up to get. We decided to go out and sell those 25 cds. This was an era when MTV cribs was on tv and things like VH1 behind the music, so we had seen artist like Scarface, Master P or Ludacris talk about selling their cds independently out the trunk of their cars, neither one of us had a car so we just threw them in a backpack and headed out.

While I was doing the 1,000 signature journey I had refined my skills to interact with strangers much more than when I went to Ohio. With my best friend being with me I felt even more prepared to get it done this time. Keep in mind neither one of us had ever sold a cd in Philadelphia before. If my memory serves me correctly we had no idea where we were headed but decided to go to South Street which is a popular spot in Philly.

While on our way we were just pitching the people we came across. I believe we took out a discman which is pretty much dinosaur talk at this day in age. A discman played cds with headphones connected to it just in case you're reading this in the year 3000. While on a train platform we spoke to 2 girls and told them what we were doing and they ended up buying it for $5, If my memory is correct, which there is a great possibility I am wrong, one of the girl's name is Amaala, who I still know until this day. We ended up talking to dozens if not hundreds of people that day and sold all the cds for $5. which we split the money evenly amongst each other. That day showed us what was possible and we would go on to do that many more times.

There is a way for me to write this from strictly an autobiographical standpoint but that is not my only intention, just take a look at the different events that shaped me to be who I am today.

January 9ᵗʰ (Gratitude)

As of now for me in the present day it is 1:55am and earlier today I was out selling my album and current project *Timeless Masterpiece*. It was 18 degrees today and when the wind blew... MY GOD (smile).

I told myself that I will truly enjoy the next vacation I take with my family when we go to a beach somewhere. Today was brutally cold but I was there by choice. I have much more money in the bank than I did from doing Christmas shopping when I told you I cleared out my account. I came back from 0 so many times throughout this journey that I feel a general sense of Wealth where I KNOW what is possible when you apply faith, persistence, respect, work ethic, along with something to offer. It is almost impossible not to generate income with applying that formula.

Today I saw homeless people in the streets (which we always see being out in the world), but I recall seeing someone laying in the middle of the sidewalk with a blanket over them. You would have to be completely insensitive and egotistical not to care about a person lying on the ground especially when it's 18 degrees outside. There is also a great amount of people who have mental illness who are incapable to function in a working-class society without a strict healthy diet or daily uses of medication. I bring this up because often when I'm outside amongst the people, I make an effort to communicate with everyone and doing so I have gotten to know lots people who are homeless. I think of this because after I make my money I leave and go home to my blessed life. This is in my heart at the moment because I see them, we all see them. For those of us who are blessed to comprehend and respond in an intelligent manner upon request we are truly fortunate. Some struggle with such ailments that it makes it extremely difficult to function and be productive in life.

I say this to you and to myself that we must be Grateful for the abilities we possess, we must honor them. Don't take these gifts in vein. If you question your gifts, please look again. If you are reading this it shows one of your greatest gifts, the ability to learn and comprehend. We as humans have to ability to program ourselves. We can learn, we can cultivate knowledge and skills. We can practice we can become better. Such a gift should not be taken for granted because there are some who unfortunately are not capable of such skills. I hope you were able to bask in the feeling of gratitude as I was able to do so in my own life through writing this.

" Working 3 jobs "

Thinking back on the journey I remember selling hundreds of Music Over Business cds with B over the weekends, around this time I was working at 3 different jobs in one day. I would wake up early and go to a Marketing Research job, leave there then go to my Telemarketing job, then make it home to rest a little bit and go to my seasonal overnight job working at Kohl's. I did that for several months. The seasonal job ended and I remember sitting at my Telemarketing job one day and saying to myself that's it. It's time to work for myself full time. It was a burning feeling in my soul like the Universe was letting me know I was ready. I remember telling B, I was about to quit my job as he was working for a wire company. This was months if not a year or two of selling the cds on the weekends. We got so good at it that I started doing it by myself on my days off and giving B a percentage of the sales because I was selling his cd. We sold hundreds and hundreds of cds. I began to get a little known in the city for being the guy with the INFITAINMENT jacket selling the cds

Inspiration to evolve

While selling Music over Business I remember hearing people say they don't listen to rap so that let me know it was time to expand and get into different genres of music. One day while I was on South street I met a Poet by the name of Elizabeth Marie. She purchased M.O.B. from me and we stayed in contact, I told her about my vision to expand musical genres and she was on board.

Tainted Lab

B had been working with a producer/engineer named Brom who at the time was running a studio named Tainted Lab. I booked some studio time and we recorded an entire cd of Elizabeth Marie and named it Ideology. We took a picture of her standing at a waterspout in Love Park and pressed up *Ideology* the poetry/ R&B album.

January 11ᵗʰ Reflection

As I sit back at 4:30am I think about how everything came together. As soon as the thought entered my mind to expand and start selling different musical genres I began to meet people who were opened to the idea of me pressing up their music. INFITAINMENT was a true record label, we definitely weren't grossing Millions of dollars, but we were creating, distributing, and promoting. A few months after selling both M.O.B and Ideology, B finished up Music Over Business 2 and we were moving forward.

I had developed a tough skin for hearing the phrase "no thanks" while selling on the streets, we created a good system. After a while when hustling you start to see the consistent faces of people who are hip to the game.

" A people in poverty long enough men acquiring riches through intelligence and not ignorance "

Being downtown you would regularly see Muslim brothas selling fragrance oils, incense, and shea butter. I would run into other music sellers like a good friend I made along the way named Apple Martini, just to give him his proper respect his name was an acronym meaning "A people in poverty long enough men acquiring riches through intelligence and not ignorance." I always thought that was cool, plus I heard him say that thousands of times. I went on to meet Maj Toure who I actually heard about while getting the thousand signatures, they called him the subway prophet because he would sell his cds on the trains. An artist named B.K. who had a cd called felony flow who had been recently released from prison and was using his music to stay in a positive direction. A Muslim Sista named Tomahawk who released a cd Hustle or Starve. Afloe/Los who was a known artist in the city because he was always in the mix. He sold mixtapes of more well-known artist around that time. Spoken Wordz who I also had met getting the 1000 signatures as she was interning working for a local record label known as Hilltop records. Last but not least A Marriage Entertainment, it was about 5 brothas in the group but you mainly saw two of them out and about marketing and selling the cds. At the time I would say they were the best because they were all over the city and had their cds professionally packaged with a barcode and everything. I saw them with a clipboard getting people for their mailing list. The two people I saw the most were named Butch and Wiz, they are legends in the game and that is why I had to mention them now.

" A street named Broad & Chestnut "

One day I was promoting the cds around downtown Philly and I saw Butch in an area of Broad street that I wasn't really familiar with. A street named *Broad & Chestnut*, he told me it was a good place to sell the cds because it was a *Tower Records* music store and other Artist seem to hang out there. The seed was planted as I continued on my journey. Not only did I see the positive hustles at work I saw the illegal ones as well. I wouldn't have made it this far minding people's business and as long as no one was getting hurt it wasn't my place to say or do anything.

One big hustle I saw were people selling bootleg cds and dvds. Daily people would ask me if I had some of the latest music and movies for sale and after a while I thought it wouldn't be a bad idea to start making copies of the bootlegs I was able to purchase which was a huge mistake. The old saying goes supply and demand and when it was all said and done I was making over $500 dollars each time I went out to sell those bootleg dvds.

It didn't take long for the Universe to show me that I was getting on the wrong track when I got in trouble with the police for having them on South street one day. I actually got roughed up a little in the process because of my big mouth, my face was rubbed in the concrete which I still have the scar to this day, while getting handcuffed my arm twisted so far that I thought it was going to break. The situation could have went another way if I would have been wise enough to keep my mouth shut. I was actually given the opportunity to walk away and just have all the dvds confiscated, I had close to 100 of them. I was young dumb and tough for no reason and begin to tell the officer what I thought of him. He called me an ass hole as I walked away. I then told him that he was the ass hole and that's when he proceeded to place me under arrest as I resisted. I spent about a week detained and had to go through all the court stuff for years! I learned my lesson and never did anything with the bootleg stuff again.

Focus on your Positive Gifts

When you have a gift a lot of time you will get tested to be steered off track. I pray that those of you reading this book when presented with the choice to do right or wrong take council through these words and they will be enough not to be greedy, as greed takes you through a path of choices that can get you into to trouble. Watch out for the traps, anything that can take your freedom away is not worth the money you can generate. It's always risk versus reward and easy money comes and goes easily. You start to lose your identity in the long run, yes it is sometimes harder than taking the illegal route but the universe will still find a way to reward you if you utilize your gifts.

Early bird gets the worm

It's 4:53am right now as I write this, and I am preparing to get up and go to New York to work. I want to get there before the sunrise, I woke up at 3:33am and decided to write a little bit before I started my day. I am going to write this book all year but I feel it may be time to expedite its release to the public. Afloe, one of the artists I worked with in the past just released a book of his poems and rhymes from over the years and it inspired me to finish this up quicker than I envisioned.

Inspiration

I have to take this time to speak on a good brotha who inspired me to know I can write this, and his name is Lloyd Williams, I see him in New York selling his books; 1 book is called Stephanie's Diary and the other called Black Angels. He's a guy that dresses dapper and is selling lots of books hand to hand. I respect his work ethic and it was an honor to get to know him. As I write this I consider him a friend and I told him yesterday I would mention him in the book and here it is.

III

Pisces - I Believe

My Daughter Wisdom took a picture of me as I took a picture of her, I brought her a pink camera so she could start to take her own pictures due to the fact she was infatuated with the ones I owned. I figured she could create a book of pictures and tell her story as well as she grows up and keep the family business going. I recall speaking about my bank account in the first chapters, right now I have well over a thousand dollars, and I even let B hold $1,000 to be returned in about 2 weeks he is supposed to give me back $1,500 so we will all see if he pays it on time which is supposed to be on the 22nd of March. I just purchased a drone with a really good camera which allows me to capture aerial shots while doing cinematography and photography. I'm talking to B right now on the phone as I type he told me to make sure that you know that the money was used as a loan for his LLC. Sleepless Knights company which is a true legal entity. There is a lot going on right now which is great!

3-16 My Dad Woody

My fingers froze over the keyboard as I prepared to write about what is taking place in my life.

My Father Woodrow Mitchell just passed away from a Heart Attack....

The connection with my father is deep, even as I write I feel connected with him because of all the letters I written him over the years. Getting a chance to be with him in the streets feels surreal being that he spent 28 years of my life in Prison. I was there the day he got off the train, the first family member he saw in the outside along with his Sister my Aunt Jean. I have nothing but positive feelings for my father. He was and is a true O.G. my Sister Donna described him as a Man of the Street. A "Streetman"... To me he was my Dad and to my Brother John the same. I have two other brothers Nate and Michael who didn't get a chance to speak with him much once he came home from prison. My Dad has so many Grand and Great Grandchildren that he said he would live forever, and that he most definitely will...

When it rains it pours

Not only was my Father's death enough to deal with while driving I was rear ended and in banged up in 4 car collision. Everyone walked away which is a blessing, I have a cousin named Donovan who died in a car accident, and for a second I didn't know how many crashes I was going to hear. I didn't know if a big truck was coming next. It was a crazy situation to be in while on my way to visit my father in the hospital. So if ever I had to think positive the time is now.

Converting negative to positive

It's not hard to give advice or provide emotional support, but when it's time to offer the same amount of support to yourself, will you be able to do so. A part of myself feels destructive but I told my Brother John the same thing I'm telling you and myself, we must be constructive and not destructive. Hence why I am writing about it at this very moment. A part of me wants to sit around and sulk it all in and do nothing, but I will convert the energy and be productive. I suggest the same for you in your life. **When** the time comes and life shows you who's really the boss and you have to deal with death, illness, or some other type of trauma, the energy of the event must be distributed somewhere positive.

We all must continue to move forward but never be too busy to experience emotion

Some people start drinking more alcohol /using drugs, some start eating more, while others may hide in work and keep themselves overly productive to mask the pain. We all must continue to move forward, but never be too busy to experience emotion. Right now there is a wave of emotions hitting me. I choose to stay away from the victim role too long, especially with my 3-year-old Wisdom and my wife to be Kristen in the picture. So as I enter into this next part of life, now without a living mother or father, I am fueled with the memories of the past, and grateful for the present. Life is still good because there is life, there is consciousness with full control over our physical vessel. Oh how we are blessed to be able to do so… Being able to make a choice of which direction to go is a true blessing. There is so much to be grateful for at all times in some manner. I take a deep breath to take it all in and continue to share it with you.

Take Control of your life

After a while from writing I feel it can become a bit redundant, the main thoughts I hope to share with you is the ability to take control over your life, of course meaning those things that we can control. Thoughts are powerful things, they can literally shape our destiny. Just as we eat nutritional foods, we must take the time to digest nutritional content. There must be a way to draw strength in times of need. It's like a water well, which is an old concept but I'm sure you're familiar. I know these vibrations begat life and personal growth. For me these are trying times in one perspective because of the death of my Father combined with the car accident I was in. For a moment I prepared myself to die not being sure what else I was going to feel when I got hit. My brain was envisioning a big tractor truck coming, I had no idea what was going to happen next. I wouldn't say my life flashed before my eyes, but time slowed down and I had a multitude of thoughts in such a short moment. I find the therapy of witting to be very useful and I hope it's conveyed to you properly if ever you find yourself in need to get some of the weight off your shoulders.

V

Gemini – I Think

There is an old saying that ideas come a dime a dozen and of course the idea of writing a book is always a good one regardless of who the author is. When you begin to write a book, it is a challenge itself because there is always the doubt within yourself that thinks, "perhaps what you have to say won't appeal to anyone." But to finish and publish is what set's the author apart from the writer. I myself wear so many hats that I had to pause everything I was doing to get back to writing. Now you can't tell of course but even the last sentence I wrote was done 24 hours ago.

I always thought I was a good multitasker but now I'm starting to see the harm of doing too many things at once. At this very moment my daughter is next to me so I'm being a Dad, editing a music video on one screen of my computer, and writing to you on another. I once heard the expression "How bad do you want it", and I must say I want to be an author. I am an author... But in order for that to be a complete reality I must finish what I started, and I hope the energy of me doing so assist you in doing the same in your own life regardless of what the vision is. Now I have to get back finishing this music video I got paid to do. Excuse me

Accepting help
July 5th

So much has taken place since the last time I wrote. At this very moment it is 1:55am. It's funny I'm actually getting officially married on the 7th which is the day after tomorrow. "Wish me luck"! The other day my soon to be Mother in law Kathy said that my 3-year-old daughter Wisdom may need a speech therapist; please know this is a very intimate matter to me but I share it with you to give you the raw emotion I am feeling at this very moment. To me I look at my daughter as growing up and yes, I do believe she can enunciate her words better but being so close to her I can see her improvements. I imagine no parent wants to hear something like that, but I told her Grandparents I would work more closely with strengthening the way she says her words.

" Unique New York "

One of the exercises consist of saying *"Unique New York"* once I saw somewhere a news reporter saying those words before they went on air to prepare their diction. I am a little apprehensive about the idea of my daughter seeing a speech therapist at this point, but my wife made a statement to me that stuck in my mind, she told me that the fact I don't accept help from others too much is one of the reasons why my business is not flourishing as much as it could. I've heard someone say that a relationship can show you things about yourself that you may not be able to see. I will take those words and keep them with me, perhaps it is the Ego that blocks the help.

I share this with you as I began to bring this book to a close. We all have an ego which is described as "The I" but there are times that if we look too closely at "I" it can cause someone to make bad decision, allow me to elaborate. Within my mind I am saying "My" daughter does not need a speech therapist because she is "my daughter". Often in life you have to look outside yourself and do what is best for the situation. I am extremely proud of my daughter Wisdom and enjoy watching her grow up. I will monitor the situation and if I don't see any improvement I will not let my ego stop me from doing what is best for her. I hope the same for you in your life. If by any chance someone reveals something to you that may be constructive for your betterment, be open to what they have to say and utilize the energy to grow.

VI

Cancer - I Feel

About two weeks ago I got a text saying that my comrade Brandon "B. Logic" had been arrested for a misunderstanding and was in need of a lawyer. I felt obligated to contribute to some of the fees for the sake of friendship. I believe everyone deserves at least one bail out plus I had money sitting in the bank, so I figured what type of friend would I be if I didn't, plus he paid me back the money I loaned him a few months back. He is home now and I do expect the money back, but I won't hold it over his head.

At this point in my life I want to make the best choices for myself and family, so I avoid "virtually" all kinds of trouble. I've been using the phrase Square Up a lot lately meaning it's time to live a clean, honest, safe and trouble-free life. My mind is consumed with thoughts of growth and development that I find it a little hard to speak to my brotha B. Logic as much as I once did. When we were younger we had many creative ideas and the biggest thing that stopped us were the resources, now that we are at the age to be able to gather the resources, I feel like this is the time to fly and fulfill anything that can be imagined. Sometimes I feel like I'm frozen in a childlike way of thinking asking myself do adults still get to imagine as I recollect to a quote I once heard saying that **the artist is the child who survived**.

Time Traveler

I recently just paid an artist by the name of Rob Woods illustrate one of my songs into a comic book and it turned out phenomenal. I have to let it be known about the professional job he did to bring such a vision to life. The amount of detail that he put into the project exceeded my expectations. His contribution took my Art and vision to another level and I am forever grateful. That is one of the most rewarding feelings I have found about submerging myself in the world I'm in. I get to work with Superman and rarely do I have to deal with the disguise of Clark Kent, I get to deal with artist and entrepreneurs as they strive to be who they are. Within me is a desire to keep the fire burning within others and it is a big reason why I do what I do and why you are reading this today. (**see page 127**)

Cultivation 7-16

3:33am on the dot and here I am again writing and here you are reading, I don't imagine everyone who has this book will take the time to read it in its entirety. Yesterday was my first day back to work and I am officially a married man, Someone noticed me wearing my ring and asked me what is the key to a good successful marriage, I have barely been married for a week but I thought the answer I gave was pretty good and spot on, I told him the key was cultivation, In my mind I can visualize land and on the land I see tall weeds and wild bushes, but I also see the land is bearing fruits and vegetables. Both husband and wife must be willing to work on and remove the things that are not good for the relationship. I brought my crap and my wife has hers but in order for us to maintain and grow, we have to cultivate the relationship/marriage. It's a nonstop process and I'm up for the work and the harvest of happiness that comes with it.

The Next Investment

At this very moment my heart is racing, I am investing so much money into the next phase of my business ventures. For almost 15 years now I have been in the cd/dvd disc business. Most people that have met me over the years saw me selling disc I pressed up using a cd duplicator and a printer, I have sold over 50,000 of them. I want to take the time to show my appreciation in you reading this right now, because this book is a part of a long overdue evolution that needed to take place. Without people like yourself it would have been a waste, I am literally once again clearing out my bank account to take things to the next level. Along with the investment of professionally printing up this book, I have decided to focus on clothing apparel as well. I just invested in a hat heat pressing machine to go along with the shirt heat press I have. I am taking the brand of Timeless Masterpiece and I'm going all in.

The Power of Investing

I've learned investing is what separates the dreamers from the doers in the world. You must be willing to invest the time & money to turn your dreams into reality.

They say the definition of insanity is doing the same thing repeatedly and expecting a different result. If you have an idea or a vision you have to go for it. I pray that you find the courage to believe that your ideas can become reality. Perhaps our thoughts and ideas are a map to fulfill our destiny. Who determines if that idea will become successful or not, if you are looking anywhere outside of yourself then that is step number 1.

You have to believe that you are worthy to achieve. I know people that would find everything wrong before they attempted to see any results, these people are generally referred to as being pessimistic. There is nothing wrong with understanding the obstacles that may lie within your way, in fact it is actually wise to do so. The moment you sit among your own thoughts and conceptualize failure instead the necessary steps to succeed, you are defeated. What is life without hope and the challenge to manifest a vision? How empty would the world be if no one thought the impossible was possible? Only those who dare know the feeling of such an achievement and I choose to be amongst them, do you

VII

Leo – I Will

On August 11th 3:24am I just wanted to be able to sleep, it would have been great to say something poetic, but the words are not revealing themselves at the moment. My wife and daughter are of course sound asleep in the other room. I have several things on my mind that need to be accomplished but my main focus is editing two videos that I have been compensated to create. Everything else; besides taking care of home business is secondary. I made some great investments to be able to start manufacturing Timeless Masterpiece shirts and hats.

I'm proud to say that I made my first hat sales August 9th in New York .The first person to purchase a hat was a brotha that goes by the name JML, coincidently he is featured in one of the first commercials I created to promote the Timeless Masterpiece album. I paid him $20 about 6 months ago because I thought it turned out pretty good. He saw me the other day with the hat's and was honorable and purchased a hat from me for $20. This dude is what we call a Cannon in the hood, he's a tough guy and I've seen him show it on many occasions in the streets of New York. Since I've been coming to the city he has showed me nothing but respect, perhaps it's simply because that's what I have been showing him. We have conversations about what it means to be a Moor,

Noble Drew Ali, and greet each other on the square by saying Islam.

The second person to get a hat is a Sista by the name of Sabrina Mason. I told her I would write about her because she is the first person to do the package deal I envisioned. She got the Timeless Masterpiece album, the dvd, the digital version sent to her phone, a wristband, hat, and a "prestige" bag with our logo for $50, we call that the platinum package. The Diamond Package is coming soon which will be a $100 but first I must finish this book. This is truly a new age to embark upon because I have been committed to selling media on disc for over 15 years now. Music and film are great but with the surge of the internet and streaming content right on the phone, the disc is now outdated and really just takes up space at this point.

I also met a couple who I introduced myself to and the guy was open to getting two hats for $30 being that it was the first day I was willing to accept it because it's still a fairly good profit. I turned my back to get the hats not taking the money first and the guys girlfriend must have quietly talked him out of it. I was disappointed but I found enjoyment in it for some reason, He then said he would get one hat for $15 but me being a salesman wanted him to do $20, not so much for the money but for the sport of sales I went for it. He ended up not buying anything because he then wanted to then give me $10 for the hat, I then retorted to a lesson I learned years ago when a person told me **1 bird in the hand is better than 2 in the bush**, meaning that sometimes you have to close or settle on an offer that is present because there is a possibility you may end up with nothing as I did. I still managed to get something from the situation and find value in the experience because here it is before you today.

At this moment it's 4:42 and my computer is about to die and instead of plugging it in I figure now is a good time to try to get some sleep wake up and finish the videos I have to do.

Bigger On The Inside

It's 7am and I'm up early to finish a Short Film/Music Video I recorded that should've been finished by now. The guy who wrote and directed the project wants to make it as close to perfect as possible which I can respect. His name is Cleous GloWry Young, and you may hear his name again in life because he's working diligently and keeps the Most High in the forefront of what he does which generally a recipe for success. I could keep writing about this but there is something else on my mind I want to get to.

August 21st Solar Eclipse

All over the news and social media I have been hearing about the solar eclipse coming up today, the last solar eclipse of this magnitude took place before I was born over 30 years in 1979. It's cool because my Mother and Father were here and I wasn't even thought of, and here I am preparing to see it with my daughter Wisdom. My wife is really into Social Media, so she told me that there were a lot of people looking for the special glasses that are needed to view the solar eclipse. She informed me that the glasses were at the 7-11 convenience store around the corner from us that had them for $7.99.

Seeing the demand for the solar eclipse glasses we came up with the idea to buy and resell them to the people who were searching online. (Hey it's America, that's how the game is played). I went and purchased about 10 of them so I spent a little less than $80, I kept 2 pair for myself and daughter because my wife has to work when the eclipse is scheduled to take place . To get to the point we took those $7.99 glasses and posted them online 1 for $25 2 for $40 with free delivery in the area. We quickly sold the first set and so did 7-11 so the glasses were becoming hard to come by. Everyone was selling out of the glasses which started out at $2. if not free in some cases but since a lot of people were not that interested in the eclipse at first, we all waited for the last minute, so the prices went up. Finally, we found the glasses again and I invested in another 10 pair. My wife said she would not put up any money but she would post them online and take a $5 commission off each one that sold. We sold all 10 throughout the day. Yesterday we said we would do it one more time but this time they were even harder to find, the price was now $15.00 per pair which were being sold in a what some may say " a bad neighborhood" in Elizabeth Nj. Now I'm from Philly so I never have a problem going anywhere through the grace of God, not because I'm some big tough guy, I just have a vibe that sticks with me from growing up in Philly.

I saw how people were responding to my wife's post, so I took the chance and invested $300 to get 20 pairs of glasses. Since the prices went up for us, as did our prices that we posted online. We sold the glasses 1 for $30 2 for $55 . Within the hour someone needed 2 but wanted to get a deal for 4 so we sold them 4 for $100. The next person was referred by the purchaser who was a cool Jewish guy named Jeremy who lived in a $800,000-dollar home. I only know because my wife looked up the house (she does stuff like that). The person he referred was named Brad who wanted to buy 8 glasses and he was prepared to pay $30 for each. With that sale for $240 I made my money back plus a $40 profit and the rest of the sales would be all profit. The last sale came at 10:30pm last night which was 2 for $55, We were SOLD OUT. It was a great experience to do with my wife because I literally didn't sell one of them. It also opened my eyes of new ways of thinking to generate revenue.

" the best way to make money is to Solve a Problem. "

For over a decade the only way I was interested in making money was through my business INFITAINMENT and an occasional paid survey here and there. Often I hear people say there is no jobs and no opportunities; let this little story confirm that there is ALWAYS an opportunity or a way to make money in life, especially in this beautiful corporation we call the U.S . Opportunity is a matter of thought and perception and like my instructor, Mr. Earl Boyd once told me, **the best way to make money is to Solve a Problem**.

VIII

Virgo – I analyze

Right now it is 9:02am and I am on a train to New York. Normally I'm listening to music when I'm on my way to work but I left my headphones. A few years back while working in NY I tried to sell a guy one of my cds, he didn't buy one but I gave him my business card. His name is BaseMan Dave and he has been getting Music Videos done by me every other month. The encounter when we first met didn't turn into an immediate benefit but the seed that was planted germinated and began to bear fruit.

The other day when he dropped of an envelope filled with the images he wanted in the video along with a payment, he stuck around for a little bit as he usually does. That's when another gentleman approached wearing a suit without a tie and said he has been seeing me for a while. To make a long story short he said that he was the Vice President of Sony which is a record company /movie company. On top of that he looked at BaseMan Dave and said he remembered his face from somewhere. Come to find out he "said" he recognized him from being in the army while they were in Germany.

Now I don't know for sure if all this information is true. I looked him dead in his eyes and he appeared to be straightforward. In life we can't be too gullible because there are evil people in this world who are very persuasive and lie just because they are good at it. You never know who's who, so we should never put too much trust in someone where it can turn out to be detriment to yourself or family especially in those who have not proven to be trustworthy. Don't make spontaneous decisions unless you can afford the disappointment. I don't know if anything will come from meeting the Gentleman whose name was something like David Baughman, but I can tell you that he looked me right in my eyes and said he knew I was going to be successful. If I don't believe anything else he said I believe that 100%...

6:56pm - After Work

I'm back on the train after a horrible day in Sales, which really isn't common but days like this keep me humble and grateful. The gentleman David who claimed to be the Vice President of Sony said the other day that he would return today at 3pm which I really didn't expect him to. While I was in the middle of speaking to someone I turned around and he was there at 2:58pm. I must say I was a little shocked. He said he had a few ideas and asked me what it is I wanted to do. I told him I want to assist people in helping their dreams come true. Because that is the foundation of what my business is based on. I told him that I had a movie idea and I wanted to put *Timeless Masterpiece* in its entirety to the masses. He proceeded to say that we will have lunch on Thursday at 1:00pm. I then asked do I need to bring my 45 or my 357 he then said people like us don't need it.

September 7th

10:05 am and I'm back on the train to New York. It's business as usual as I anticipate the 1pm meeting. Perhaps nothing will come from it or perhaps today will be a life changing day we shall see. It's good for the book if anything, in life we have to do our best and let God take care of the rest. I will do my part by showing up and pray the best possible outcome, I'm looking forward to letting you know the what happened…

September 11th

First and foremost, I'm sure you know the significance of the date and with respect I decided not to go physically to work outside in New York City. I have done so before and have felt an unsettledness while I worked even though it has been almost 20 years the planes flew into the twin towers. I can't imagine what it felt like for the people that were there and the many people effected, I pause and share my thoughts and condolences…

Dedication

Right now it is 12:57am my wife was a little upset with me that I came in the house a little before 12am from working late night in front of Madison Square Garden, but I wanted to reach a certain quota before I left, which I end up doing so being $10 off my goal but it was late and I knew it was time to get home. The gentleman I was supposed to have the meeting with the other day never showed up, but I do know that things happen and I haven't completely written him off yet. Who knows what the future may hold but I am not waiting for a person to come along and "discover" me which I know is possible because sometimes all it takes is the right cosign then BOOM you are to the moon and back. I am enjoying the journey of building the business and learning as I go.

The Possibilities

All kinds of interesting things happen on the journey and surely, I don't take the time to write them all. Some moments will simply live happily in my memories. The other day I had the opportunity to meet with an amazing artist name SoSo who does some incredible paintings and art. I believe earlier in the book I spoke about having the idea to create a painting that I will price at One Million Dollars. I wanted to write it out, but let me write the numbers as well, that's $1,000,000. It's a detailed piece that I know he would be great to work on with. He lives in California I believe, but I met him in New York. He purchased the Timeless Masterpiece album from me and he is interested in partnering up and doing the work. I sent him an email to follow up on my end, let's see what he does.

Passion

I've learned that we must always put the ball in others court and that is one of the best ways to build on working with others. I hope writing these things encourages you to do what you are PASSIONATE about, as I write my eyes are becoming heavy. Believe it or not I do sleep, it feels good to work all day doing my best and not just working to make money but to be a good person as well. I take great pride on building up others and encouraging as many people as I can. Why? Because it is my passion.

Speak Life

Today I was about to attempt to sell a woman one of my projects, but I notice how easily she came to speak with me, and let me tell you, at this very moment I have a full beard and I haven't gotten my haircut in about a month. I may not look like the most pleasant person to speak with but yet she was open to engage. After noticing how open she was I felt the need to let her know that I appreciated her willingness to communicate with a stranger such as I. Whatever I was saying struck a nerve and she began to cry, I translate it to her being able to hear the spirit of God behind my words, I hear it in others as well. I can't speak for you, but I know I have the ability to speak on the behalf of the Universe. I don't do this for my personal gain but when I feel compelled to do so I speak the truth from my perspective. This is not to brag or toot my own horn but it is a responsibility that some of us, if not all have been entrusted to do before the world.

You may have someone in your life whether it's a friend, family member, or even a complete stranger that you are drawn to speak to or even help. A big part of the world's problems is that too many people mind their business. You never know how your words of kindness and understanding may affect an individual. I know of a Brotha who goes by a few names and he just had a daughter; the baby has not been in the world for 2 weeks and him and the mother are having problems. Should I mind my business, or should I do my best to encourage him to get the blessing that comes with being a Father and enduring the hardships that come with co-parenting at times. I choose the latter. I am not a saint, nor do I think I am holier than thou, but as I said, I take on the responsibility of being the brightest light I can be in this world. It's not about being perfect it's just about having the courage to know that each one teaches one, and Iron sharpens Iron. BE GREAT I'll holla back, it's time for me to get some sleep.

" perfection is upon the beholder "
9/20 12:48 am

When I first started writing one of the biggest reliefs was not to be over critical of myself and attempt to make everything perfect which is virtually impossible. I assume inwardly that perfection is upon the beholder which makes me think of an artist named Ben who I met the other day. I was posted outside Madison Square Garden on my usual square both literally and figuratively when I saw Ben with a hand full of his art on several canvases. I didn't make any money yet that day and I only had $10 cash on me. Often I try to be to others that I look for the Universe to send me from time to time. People who will just buy from me just because. So without Ben the Artist saying anything, I asked if his artwork was for sale. He said to me that it was not finished. I looked over a few pieces and said they look finished to me which they did. I saw a painting that had various colors and was somewhat pinkish so I asked him if I could give him the $10 for it. I told him it was for my daughter Wisdom, so he was more open to letting it go for such a price. Ben appeared to be homeless but Hell, I guess I might appear to be to some people as well at times; being that I'm always outside and selling things. He signed the painting on the back to Wisdom, "May you always discern" which I thought was great to write. He added a few more things to his artwork as we made conversation and he walked off.

What we see and what others view is not always the same. I felt I was done with this book months ago because I made so many points and shared so many experiences, but I felt I wanted to write throughout the rest of the year to make it complete. Generally I don't do kind acts to get kind acts returned to me, I just do them because that's what I feel like doing. I found value in showing as much kindness to people as I can and to those who are struggling in various matters.

Mr. Josh Kearse

I've been thinking to myself that there are people who live their lives looking to be a blessing as much as they can in some shape or form. There is a gentleman by the name of Josh Kearse who works inside MSG and every chance he gets he ask me if I want something to drink. He introduced me to Kombucha Drink which you have to do your own research on because I don't feel like getting too sidetracked. There are others who offer me something to drink as well but he generally makes it a routine at this point. Special thanks to Mr. Josh Kearse for showing the world the kindness of which I speak.

" Branding and Marketing "
1:17am

Fall is approaching and it's starting to get cooler outside, earlier in the day I purchased a new jacket that I wanted to get an all-black bomber. I've been feeling artistic so I turned it into a Timeless Masterpiece Jacket. It turned out pretty good, I'm in a stage where I'm doing really good with branding and marketing and here is a brief list of a few things that I have done so far.

Timeless Masterpiece
Album
Visual Album
Documentary
Wristbands
Hats
Shirts
Stickers
Bags
Water Bottles
Book
Jacket

I don't want to do too much but that might be plenty, who knows what else I might get inspired to do. I'm also planning to do my own tie line which I plan on calling "Inf Mitchell" coming so soon that I even purchased my Suit jacket today. I find myself investing a lot of the money back into my businesses to keep expanding. The other day a guy came up to me and said he has some old albums he wanted to sell me. I took it as a sign from the universe because I want to make a painting involving different music mediums such as cassette tapes, cds, and albums. I was planning to get someone else who actually has skills with drawing but perhaps I will take it as a sign to do it myself. The few artists I reached out to are a little too hesitant for me, so even as I write I am getting more motivated to do the 1 Million dollar painting myself. There is a huge doubt going on in my mind saying, "nobody is going to buy a painting from me for 1 Million Dollars, I can't draw or paint". Doubts will always exist, but what matters in the end is if you allow yourself to succumb to those poisonous thoughts... I'm looking forward to creating the painting MY WAY...

Losing Loved Ones
September 22nd

I woke up about 6am with a lot on my mind as I prepare to take my wife and daughter to my Aunt Bernice's funeral. Within the past 6 months I lost my Father, my Uncle Joe, and just within the past week my Aunt Bernice. 3 siblings and the person I feel for the most is my Aunt Jean who had to watch 2 of her brothers go and now her sister, she still has one sister alive which is my Aunt Loretta who we call Auntie. My cousin Fran and Aunt Jean want me to record the service so I am going to do it for them. Since I am going to take my camera I am planning to get some of my Brothers and Sister to speak about my Father, Mom, and myself for my upcoming documentary.

IX

Libra - I Balance

September 30th 10:13am

On the train once again to New York, I was in my hometown of Philadelphia yesterday and had an amazing day. I was received with open arms and a lot of people were happy to see me and support the business. The feeling was unique, it was not overwhelming but I felt how it could have gone to my head. I felt extremely blessed and my ego had to be contained which I felt like only God could do.

Early that day I picked up at least 100 cds and a few dozen cassettes from my cousin Felisa which was her and her brother's my cousin Bubby who died about 20 years ago . I plan to add the cds and tapes for the *Timeless Masterpiece Sculpture/Painting*. I have so much to write about but I'm about to get off the train and get to work. I was listening to TD Jakes a pastor/motivational speaker and he said something that stuck out to me and I will share it with you, say this with me before I get off the train and get to work. Say " I DESERVE TO BE BLESSED!!".

Mission Minded
October 1st 3:33am

I woke up about 10 minutes ago when I felt that I couldn't go right back to sleep once I heard my daughter Wisdom call me to get her to take her to the bathroom, I knew it was time to get up and write. My wife then called out asking me "what was I doing?" As I began to type I told her adding to my book, I then heard her sigh then go back to sleep. In life we must be mission minded which is the only way to manifest a vision. We all are capable of achieving great things but it really comes down to how bad you want it. One of the biggest songs that motivated me in life was *I Believe I Can Fly* by **R. Kelly**. I won't go quoting the words or anything but look it up if you need to. We have to be able to fuel the fire and the universe will provide such fuel if you keep moving forward and if you are willing to listen to the signs, hence how my daughter Wisdom called me while I was awake.

I am actually a little tired so here are a few things I want to hit on before I go to sleep and get ready for the work day in a few hours.

Thank you Catherine

I've really expanded the brand by adding hats and the T shirts, the shirts say Once Upon A Timeless Masterpiece and the hats have the logo, while presenting the album , dvd, into a custom professional white bag that also has the logo on there. I offer that entire package for $50 a young lady by the name of Catherine Janke in New York City was the first person to do the entire package and I told her I would mention her in the book.!

Thoughts become things

A beautiful thing to perceive is that I am simply selling thoughts that have been converted into something tangible. ANYONE can manifest their thoughts into reality; as I have a flashback of being a child for some reason. Perhaps we are only as special as we believe ourselves to be, perhaps our destiny is cultivated from various seeds planted and by those who water them along the way. Maybe it's fate or something genetic within our DNA, or an astronomical connection magnetically guiding us.

Meeting Jeremy Van Tress

While working I saw a guy riding in a motorized wheelchair; I tend not to discriminate as I try to treat each person the same regardless. Unless I assume a person is too young, too old, or have a real mental challenge I'll attempt to sell any and everybody. The gentleman stopped as I gave him my sales pitch, he was open to patronizing the business as I notice how bright his light was. He told me he has *Lou Gehrig's disease* also known as ALS, a disease that affects muscles and nerves. He said he had a bucket list because it can be fatal in time. As I type I feel for him and can't imagine myself or loved ones having to go through it. I heard him talking and he sound like he had so much to share, something told me to give him my phone and let him write whatever he wanted to share, and this is what he wrote which I have not read yet.

"I am pleased to give my voice to the people who may see my words. I am a 35-year-old Amy Veteran and social worker. I am suffering with ALS and terminal neurodegenerative disease. I am the happy husband and father to 6 beautiful children. I have been around the world in various capacities in my life. What I wish to share with others is simple. Be good to one another. Love others and embrace life for the good of everyone. Life is short- make it count not just for yourself, but for everyone you meet. May God bless everyone who reads this!"

Much Love and respect to brother Jeremy and his family...

" I created a challenge for myself "
October 1st 4:03pm

At this very moment I'm on the train after selling all my products and making my quota and in the immortal words of Ice Cube, *"Today was a Good Day"*. A unique event happened while I was at work attempting to sale my last *Timeless Masterpiece hat* to a gentleman who goes by Coach Ray Lilley. He spoke as if he was a wealthy man while smoking his cigar while observing me. He didn't buy my last hat which was fine, but I became a little frustrated because he saw how hard I was working as he continued to make conversation. Knowing myself I felt if the situation was reversed I would've purchased whatever the young man was selling if I was going to critique. I told him to stick around and to step to the side as I sold the last one. I asked him to give me a time limit to sell the last hat which he then challenged me to sell it in 7 minutes. I then glanced across from me and noticed a young man watching. He was wearing a Bob Marley t shirt with locs in his hair. As he walked over I told him all we had left was one hat which he purchased for $16 I gave it to him even though the price of the hat was $20. The young man's name is Chad Griffiths from Jamaica.

I created a challenge for myself and was able to deliver in 30 seconds. I share these things with you not to boast in my ego alone "you feel me" but to show the power of thought. The same thought power we all possess especially if you were able to read this book. You must be special in some shape or form, because only great men and women work to refine themselves and work towards unlocking their potential or becoming better than they were yesterday. I sit on the train a champion, victorious in the mission I set out to accomplish. There were times in my life when I didn't know how I was going to make it, but God…

Interactions
October 4th 2017

Before I start typing too much about what's really on my mind, I want to take the time to thank Miss Syreeta Brown who was the first person to get the $50 package in Philly. Another person I want to mention is a young man named Alan Laco who I often see in New York in the streets. I complimented him on his watch as he froze engulfed in his own thoughts then took it off and gave it to me. I know him as being homeless and maybe going through his own personal struggles or addictions, but he has always been cool just seeing him pass by. I asked him why he chose to give me the watch and he simply replied something told him to do it. It's not about the cost of the watch, and I'm pretty sure I will never wear it, but it does look nice so for him to give it to me it is special. One more thing about the watch is that it is both digital and has the clock dials on it which I personally have never owned or saw before off hand. I KNOW that I don't have to be the one to reward him for obeying the voice that told him to give me the watch. The universe rewards people who give, especially those who don't look for anything in return. I will be sure to return the generosity to him when the time presents itself. I told him that I would write about him and if it was anything he wanted to share. He began to shed tears... He appreciated the fact that I was talking to him because he sees that I'm focused and about my business but he appreciated the fact that I was able to communicate with him and not act above him just because of how I present myself. In all honesty I believe that all of us as human beings should take the time to look at one another and acknowledge one another. It might make a positive impact in the world if we are willing to take the responsibility to know that our actions can make a difference beyond just that one person we interacted with...

Investing in a Vision
4:40pm

I had a little over 2 thousand dollars saved up to invest in this book or for a rainy day. I ended up Investing all of it within the past two days. I have been finding success with the clothing apparel, so I but a huge chunk into that to keep it going. I paid some bills to be ahead, got my wife a nice bag for her birthday, I ordered 1,300 Timeless Masterpiece wristbands, A lot of hats, shirts, and other materials, but my newest investment was for my painting/sculpture that I am going to sell for 1 Million Dollars. It's beautiful because I had the idea, wrote it down when it came to me about 2am and today is the day I purchased the canvas for it. I have been gathering materials for it for about a week now, and it is now a reality.

Inspired again
10-10

Currently it's 3:53am and I'm in Atlantic City, don't worry I only lost $20 of my own money on Roulette and $50 in free slot play, I have never been too lucky in that regard. I began to think to myself as I awoke out my sleep that perhaps things happen for a reason to inspire us to move in a certain direction in life, or perhaps we move where we want. In any perspective I have been inspired to paint more and do more art pieces. 1 piece I have been inspired to do will be multiple mask to symbolize the various faces we use to cover who we truly are at times. I had another that I saw visually but I forgot (that's why it is always important to write your visions down. Another was one that says Dreams, Believe, Work Hard, Achieve It, but something to add on to Timeless Masterpiece I decided to do 12 paintings each having its own Zodiac sign quoting a lyric off each song I did or depicting it some type of way. I have a cousin whose name is Kimika "Mo Mo", even though we are not blood related her work as an artist has inspired me to make these creations. I would like to thank her for manifesting her own visions into reality and being an inspiration…

Trust the Process
10-21

It's 2:32am and me being up right now is due to drinking some type of Starbucks concoction that had espresso in there because I had to ride back from Philly kind of late. To be honest I would prefer to be sleeping but since I'm up I will do my best to utilize the time wisely. Before I decided to write I thought about the reality that what you are reading is a past look at myself. My accomplishments and perception are frozen forever within this book, it can only define this particular moment in my life, by the time you have read this I will have evolved to reach higher and tackle even more. If I wrote this book 10 years ago it simply would not have as much substance as there is today, what of the next ten years, what shall I have to offer then. I share this to say that there is no better time than the present. I always refer to the book I tried to write when I was around 7 years old perhaps without that moment of boldness to create you would not be reading this book today while I am at the age of 33. It will almost be one year since I went on the journey to create this and much has happened within the year.

The fact my father was alive when I started to write is pivotal to me. I took a second to think of a moment when I sat on a bench with my daughter Wisdom as we ate our Water Ice. It was a beautiful day as we sat on the bench I looked up at the sun and all I could do was shed a tear as I shared that time with her. I shed a similar tear even now even as I write, the tear is a feeling of gratitude. I am thankful for the moments of peace I get to experience within my life.

Grateful for Peace

Within the news current events are filled with destructive hurricanes that have destroyed thousands of homes and killed hundreds in different parts of the world. Mass shootings at music concerts leaving over 50 people dead and hundreds injured. Talks of a nuclear war with North Korea, Cops killing innocent people, People killing innocent people, I could go on and on, as I'm sure you can turn on the news and see the horrible things going on currently within your reality. All that to say is as I sat there with my daughter on the bench there was NOTHING in my reality but peace. It was beautiful to comprehend as I am inspired to use that very location for future productions, if you keep up with my work and if you see any scenes of my daughter and I sitting on a bench in a park that is it.

Bilal Smith

I want to pause and acknowledge a good brotha who is another great artist I met on the journey. His name is Bilal Smith. I have known him for several years remembering our first encounter when I saw him carrying a huge Allen Iverson painting he did which was amazing. Often we crossed paths but I got to see him more at my Brotha Isaiah Ham T shirt printing company on Broad street named Statement Clothing. I am writing about him specifically today because for the past couple times I saw him while working he has spent money and patronized my business. Today he spent $30 and got a hat and shirt from me. Today I saw him point his finger and yell at this older guy for not being responsible as an elder. Bortha Bilal was talking about doing some coding with lights and electronics, and the older guy not knowing any better said "that ain't no money" which was wrong of him as an elder. He should have encouraged the young man for having a vision but he was sick mentally, so Bilal let him have it and said him and people like him failed the youth. The older guy said to Bilal "What have you done for the youth!" I answered that for him and responded each time he sees me he puts money into my business. He is making an impact for us as a people, artistically, and for the community. I appreciate him and wanted to acknowledge that I don't undermine his contributions. He is one of the great artists of our time and I 100% recognize him as so. Much Respect to Brotha Bilal Smith and Thank You!

X

Scorpio - I Desire

Something inspiring to know is that one always has the ability to evolve but also in the same light one can continue to make bad decisions and be counterproductive over time. Yesterday on the 27th of October I began to work on my sculpture. I'm proud of the progress thus far.. I want to take the time to thank a young Man by the name of Danny who spent $50 with us in New York. I've invested more money in the past 2 years than I ever have before. I'm looking forward to offering the $100 package and meeting the first person who does it to show and prove that it is possible. When you do something for the first time you just have to repeat the formula. The next attempt you make you have more of an advantage because you know what it takes.

For the first time I feel that I have outgrown being outside hustling and promoting the business, I always question the idea of opening a store. Not only do you have to pay rent, you have to get the people inside of your location, then they have to actually spend money once they get there. Of course, there is a way to do this and be successful but being outside is virtually free.

Expansion

Today I have expanded my set up yet once again with the introduction of a virtual reality unit combined with a nice-looking display. I'm waiting for my Subpac a backpack type of mechanism this allows you to feel the bass as you wear it. I figured combining it with a good pair of headphones all together would make the presentation more intriguing and interactive. I'm presently on the train a little behind schedule from working and celebrating my birthday a little early which is coming up on November 7th. I can't imagine the words that I am writing are painting a clear picture how I feel at this very moment. I feel like I have built the business to be impressive and innovative.

(Nice and Easy)
November 5th

Presently I am in the air on my way to Jamaica, my wife and daughter are sitting next to me. I am celebrating my birthday coming up on the 7th. It's cool because all 3 of us are Scorpios. I told them the motto for the trip will be "nice and easy". I figure if I say it enough it will be spoken into existence and we can enjoy ourselves. For the past couple weeks it seems as if I am getting everything I want and can imagine. You may have read other books that talk about having the power to speak things into existence and the power of thought.

Shine the Light

The law of attraction is a phrase that gets thrown around from time to time, they call it "The Secret". As I sit here literally in the sky I know that you may be reading this and I have become more successful than I possibly could have envisioned. If the Lord is willing I will live a long fruitful life and when I am dead and gone these words can still inspire and motivate to prove that you can manifest your thoughts into reality. I have my headphones in listening to Bob Marley who has been gone for many years now but yet his spirit lives on through his art. I brought my drones and cameras to shoot a video for one of my songs "Shine the Light" it's featuring an artist by the name of I.Zo who is Jamaican. I don't have a clear vision of what I want to do with the video yet but I'm looking forward to creating it.

A chance to relax
11 - 9

Right now I am overlooking the mountains in Jamaica, the water is clear and the sky is blue. It was a great vacation, I had a chance to relax and enjoy the simple things in life and appreciate them as we always should. I had a chance to visit where Bob Marley was born and where both he and his mother have been laid to rest. I appreciate being there.

Thoughts of Making History
November 12th

I feel that this has turned more into a diary than I would have liked but I hope you still manage to get something from it. At the end of the day I went forward on a journey that I didn't depart from. I always knew I wanted to make a mark in the world in some shape or form. Through television I watched, Michael Jordan, Hulk Hogan, Malcolm X, Bob Marley, and the list goes on. We watched these people as well as fictional characters like Rocky accomplish incredible things. I am a Titan and often I think of the sacrifice of the young black man Trayvon Martin who was murdered, His name shall live on just as the name Emmett Till will, we honor those names but at what price.

(Sacrifices)
11-16 1:58am

There will always be criticism in some shape or form when you walk a road less traveled. Right now I am on a couch manifesting a thought but yet from one perspective I may be on the couch too much staring at a computer screen. I find myself a loss for words at the moment perhaps because it's not the best time for me to write, but yet here we are. At this very moment I may be using this book as an escape to avoid a potential argument with my wife which is a good thing in one regard. Without going into full detail I'll make a point about what inspired me to get up and share my thoughts.

Be willing to sacrifice your own ego to win and get what you want out of life. Be strong and wise enough to see the battles ahead, there is an old expression that goes. **"You may have lost the battle, but you didn't lose the war."** Satisfying your own ego at times can cause you to feel an immediate form of gratification but in the long term you must decipher if that choice will have any lasting effect. Get what you get out of that..

November 18th
Happy Birthday Wisdom

Too much to document
November 19th 7:15pm

As I live this life and walk along the path of artistry and entrepreneurship I have realized that it is impossible to understand an individual solely based on their art and what others had to say about them. Today was an extremely windy day almost very unlikely I would make any sales, but I did and had the opportunity to meet a legendary actress. Mrs. Phylicia Rashad who acted as the wife of Bill Cosby for many years. It was like meeting royalty to be honest and I was extremely honored how humble she was. I gave her a pair of *Timeless Masterpiece gloves* which we now have available and we took a nice picture. It feels like an award from the Universe.

" Peace of Jamaica "
11-28

It's a beautiful thing to have a thought and watch it manifest, I recently completed my first real painting. I call it "Peace of Jamaica" It has actual sand from the Island and sea shells within it. It turned out pretty good and I am not in a hurry to sell it, even though I made it with the purpose for someone else to own it. I have so many different things I am looking forward to creating, from paintings, to finishing this book, to creating a few more songs and movies. Right now it's 8:11am and my daughter Wisdom is lying on me watching a movie called Home alone and I plan on making a movie with her similar in the magnitude in the future.

XI

Sagittarius - I See

December 4th 1:03am

As I reflect on the year that has passed so much has happened. The first thing that comes to mind is losing my father, I could write an entire book on that experience alone. I got married this year, and I took my business to an entire new height offering clothing apparel and writing my first book. I hope that you were able to get something out of reading what has been presented.

I am simply a person who dared to stand before the world and say this is who I am. I challenge you to do the same in whatever path you choose. Some of us are chosen to be the paint upon the canvas of the universe. We are here to inspire, we are here to create, we are here to uplift. Don't take a blind eye to the problems that we see, speak up and correct those issues with the best of your ability.

Faith

There is an expression that says, **"Do your best and let God take care of the Rest"**. I look to the Most High each day because having faith makes me a better man. It gives me the strength not to feel that the weight off life has to be endured alone. It was never about religion with me if I may write freely. I never wanted to disconnect from an individual based on their culture, or what they choose to believe in.

Definition of Timeless Masterpiece

At this very moment the moon is full and very bright they are calling it a supermoon. Gazing upon the nighttime sky seeing something of that magnitude is enough to know that life is much bigger than you and I but we are a part of it together. We exist in such a reality so I pose the question; Why limit what you can do within this gift of consciousness? Fulfil an ambition, leave no stone left uncovered if you will, inspire someone to do the same and who knows what will become from such a choice. 2pac Shakur a great artist of his time who only lived to see 25 once said, " 'I'm not saying I'm going to change the world, but I guarantee that I will spark the brain that will." I closed my eyes for a second and felt the harmonic symphony of our choices. We are all utilizing each other's ideas and seeing the manifestation which was once a thought. Truly this is a Timeless Masterpiece which we are all contributors thereof.

" take each experience and manipulate the energy to benefit you "

It felt quite poetic to feel us all connected; for better or for worse which creates an experience beyond our perception. I've learned in life you must take each experience and manipulate the energy to benefit you in some shape or form. Such a task is difficult to do if you are too invested in your emotions which are not to be undervalued by any means. Emotion is a representative of passion but yet it must be harnessed to be productive and used to move in a direction where you desire. I would have not been able to write this entire book without that understanding.

Notice how I write at obscure times in the a.m. because most of the time the inspiration to write came from a place of discomfort I may have been experiencing. I was able to take those moments and use them to my benefit by converting the energy to productivity. It makes me think of the expression, **"When life gives you lemons make lemonade"**. Often when I am selling I use real life experiences, I might say "My homie B. Logic still owes me $150. from when I helped pay for his lawyer" which is true. I use real life experiences to be relatable and human which people like to connect with.

Before I close I want to share something that my brotha B. Logic told me. He told me that he got this from somewhere else and hearing it made me a better person, so I will share it with you.

Native American Wisdom

When Native American went to capture buffalo, they would use the meat for food. They also would skin the buffalo to make clothing or blankets to keep warm. The bones were turned into weapons, the horns into instruments, perhaps the teeth into jewelry, the moral is for you get the most out of the Buffalo... For those that have an ear let them hear and apply it to their own life

When Doubt Occurs
December 5th

It's 4:44pm and I am standing on my post in New York City in front of Madison Square Garden. I have a good looking display compared to where we came from. A VR unit connected with a portable Subwoofer that you wear as a vest, so you can actually feel what you are watching and listening. A tablet connected to a poster displaying the videos I have produced over the years as that stands on a separate tripod, I have a shirt that displays Once Upon A Timeless Masterpiece, and above that 3 different styles of hats displaying the Timeless Masterpiece logo which is also on pairs of gloves that I have for sale.

Hundreds if not thousands of people have walked by me since I have started writing this and not one person has stopped to inquire about it. There is even a projector I have playing displaying another video on the ground as well and more. While I am working I do my best to speak life to almost every person I come across. I give to the poor and the other people that are selling things that walk past me. For 15 years I have been building the business but all my life I have made a great effort to show my love for humanity.

I felt the weight of my compassion and it felt almost too much to bear

I felt a little overwhelmed seeing all the people with mental illness/homeless. There is a guy who we refer to as Superman who is homeless missing an eye and has serious mental illness although he is sharp enough to ask me for a dollar or two each time he sees me. I look at him and feel for him regardless how he ended up in that situation. He has so much stacked up against him with missing teeth and all. How can he thrive or excel it "seems" as if he can only survive. I felt the sense of responsibility to look after him. How could I turn a blind eye to him having a pocket full of money as if giving him a dollar would be a detriment to me in any way. At that particular moment I felt the weight of my compassion and it felt almost too much to bear. That's when a Rasta by the name of Bengali walked by and greeted me. It's as if the Most High manifested to ensure I wasn't alone in the battle to display such kindness to the world. We spoke for a brief moment and I must be honest it was difficult to control the emotion. As soon as he left while I was writing a gentleman who appeared to be homeless by the name of Cecil Desmond Stanford came by and I acknowledged him, he is from Africa and he also began to speak about the Most High, at those moments I see the manifestation of God and how the energy reveals itself.

Snow Day
12-10-17 10:30am

Presently I am on my way to work on the train to NY, it was a snow storm yesterday but I didn't let stop me from making it to work. Doing what I do for 12 years I have learned that the weather should not stop me from working outside but yet I should embrace the season. I sold everything I had yesterday and met up with an artist by the name of BaseMan Dave who I believe I spoke about earlier in the book. He made a payment to produce another one of his videos and not only that, I had a photography gig to do later that evening in New Jersey. The Universe provides not only monetarily, but spiritually and emotionally as well. When you have the moments when you question yourself and ask how can I go onward with the journey, that's when a breakthrough is on its way. You can't take 99 steps toward a goal, it has to be 100plus. As the train approaches I encourage you to be diligent in your journey, be committed let nothing stop you. If you question yourself and feel that you are not on a journey, begin one. Set a goal no matter how great or small and Make It Happen!!!

Culture
December 12ᵗʰ 3:05am

There are thousands of people around the world that contributed to my business and some didn't even speak the same language as I did. There is a terminology known as demographic when one focuses on a particular type of people and I found that I can connect with people from around the world. The majority of these people create in some shape or form or perhaps they teach. The other day I had a farmer as a customer so I would say to a degree. we were able to relate to cultivating and growing. The people I connect with the most are compassionate, they walk down the street and don't look to avoid eye contact, they are open to be engaged, they are open to be inspired. These characteristics exceed race, gender, or economic class,

As I write I think to myself that I have a video job to do for an Indian family later today. Opportunities such as this occur when people are able to communicate with you, even though there is a slight language barrier, the power of respect overcomes the accents that stand in our way. Don't shut yourself out from connecting with people who may look differently from you, opportunities and blessings come from many areas and sometimes it will come from somewhere you least expect.

The Ankh
December 18th 7:11am

I'm the type of person that looks at the clock and see's 7:10am and writes slowly, by the time I record the time it would have been 7:11. I was born November 7th which is 11 -7. Hence the desire to document 7- 11. When I was younger I asked my Mom to bring home a cross like the one Puff Daddy had on his second album entitled *Forever*. My mom didn't buy me a cross she brought home an ankh. From there I was introduced to the Kemetic symbol originally from the artist *Erykah Badu,* which she often wore and had in her album art work.

My First Original Symbol

While watching wrestling I saw the Undertaker have his own symbol which I thought was really cool. So I combined a Seven and an Ankh together and created an original Symbol. It doesn't really have a name but more of a meaning. I have referred to it in the past as "*Sevankh*" but it means Life, Love, Health, Growth , Knowledge, Unity, and Death.

" It is within our art and creativity that allows us to live forever "

I was thinking early this morning about living life and how the Egyptian Pharaohs were onto something about living forever and the afterlife. Perhaps our reality is afterlife, and the impact you make on the world determines how long your life will be remembered. Take for instance King Tutankhamun, also known as King Tut who I'm sure you are familiar with who was born in 1341 BC.

It is within our art and creativity that allows us to live forever. It's our contribution to humanity no matter how good or bad, your name can reign heavenly or your name can reign within hell which is upon perception. That's where one may get in to their own spiritual journey to determine good from evil. Perhaps such a thing does not exist but to conclude that there is only survival. Through consciousness and the knowledge of self, one could therefore look with Wisdom to see what causes them to stumble. How easily we are influenced as humans even within a genetic molecular level. From the language we speak to the culture we view as normal. Once aware of such an influence we must program our minds strategically to what we want out of our own destiny. One of the greatest gifts a person can have is the ability to gain Wisdom through our personal experiences and the experiences of other people and things…

Seasons
December 19th 8:27pm

There are scriptures in the Bible under Ecclesiastes 3 that says that **there is a season for everything**. I encourage you to read it for yourself if you feel compelled to do so. There are times when I feel very confident and I stand before the world and I'm ready to take on whatever comes my way. Today is one of those days when I didn't feel so strong, I felt the fatigue of the mental marathon of being self-employed, the marathon of living the life as an artist, the weight of choosing my creativity as my career. I embrace this brief season because it allows me channel alternative thoughts. It's easy to tell someone else how to get through their problems but the test comes when you have to take your own advice.

Tis the Season
December 25th 9:40pm

When I was younger I remember believing in Santa Claus and expecting gifts to be under the Christmas tree. My mother made sure every year I had great holidays. This is my first holiday not having either one of my parents alive. You tend to look at life differently when you lose those closest to you, well I do anyway…

It's beautiful to watch the joy of my daughter Wisdom on holidays such as Christmas. I take a long pause choosing my next words carefully, the only thing playing on repeat is the word gratitude. I am grateful, we should all find a way to acknowledge the greatest gift which is existence. The more grateful you are the less room you have for unhappiness.

I hope these words find you in a place of happiness regardless of what season you are in. Inner peace is essential to obtain such happiness and I've learned if you focus too much on other people you may find yourself unhappy depending on the situation. I close my eyes and I project happiness, I project peace, if you're up for it take a deep breath and do it with me, say I am at peace, and I am happy. For me at this time I had to do that to truly experience the feeling of happiness.

In all honesty there are things occurring in my life that if I focused on them too long I would find myself in an unhappy place. I take a moment to reflect and know for sure I have so much to be grateful for. So I share this with you; be sure to focus on the things that bring you peace and focus on those things you can control that bring forth happiness.

December 27th 1:41am

Today was a very productive day, I almost finished my entire sculpture/painting . I just completed some new *Timeless Masterpiece clothing apparel* and before the year is out I will be submitting the trademark for the *Timeless Masterpiece logo*. Overall it has been a very good year for business, in fact the best year I've had since working for myself. I'm falling in and out of sleep as I write so I better get some shut eye and get ready to go face the cold weather tomorrow at work. I'll be sure to let you know how it turns out,

The Test
December 30th 11:16am

Throughout the journey of life there will be various test we encounter regardless if we are aware of them or not. This test will come to challenge our self-control as well as other virtues. As I get older I've learned that we will not all face the same challenges. We are not here to accomplish the same goals. Everyone does not have that chosen responsibility placed upon there life. If you have been chosen to read this book I Imagine you are one of us.

Beyond the label how "we" choose to refer or define ourselves, it is a calling on your life to make an impact. This impact does not have to be grandiose, perhaps it is something within reach. A simple phone call you need to make, a conversation that needs to be held with a loved one. Perhaps it's giving away some of your old clothes and shoes to a needy family. No matter what your test may be, I am simply here to motivate you to make the choice to shine the light. As we go forth with such understanding we should not judge or look down on others because their perception of life is not the same as yours.

This is a test within our own vanity

I have learned that the greatest test that comes with talent or the "feeling" of being exceptional is the battle with the ego within. I speak on this because I too have felt the arrogance that comes with talent, I have seen it with various artist that I have worked with over the years. We are all a composition of various influences throughout our journey. When we are born we are brought in to the world from the choices of our parents, they are our first teachers, our siblings, aunts, uncles, cousins, and grandparents. The friends that we are allowed to have at the young age shape who we are. The content we are allowed to view molds us, the books, music and films teach us culture. For those of us that may have come to realize that we are all influencing each other along the way. To deny the influence is to deny the responsibility we have to humanity. We are all connected so I pose the question where will you lead us…

Time to Level Up
December 31st 1:02pm

As the classical music plays through my headphones while I'm on my way to do a music video for a young Hip Hop artist named Oddboy Roy, I'm appreciative that I am not outside vending my works on this 15-degree cold day. I always like to work on New Year's Day/eve to set the tone for the new year. I have not made any resolutions but I have some set goals in mind. First on my list is to trademark the *Timeless Masterpiece logo* I have the money to do so set aside in my bank account, I have copyrighted works but no intellectual property such as a trademark. I feel this is a step in the right direction to taking my business to the next level. The beautiful part is that I am not exactly sure where the next level is, but this book is a part of it. I know I need to set bigger goals.

Are the goals you're looking to accomplish big enough?

This will be the final day of documenting my journey this year, I must say thank you for being a part of this with me. This book means nothing much without you. I hope you have taken something away from what I have wrote and shared. Although I have always had a certainty of my success it is still yet a vision, a work in progress. Though I feel successful in some regards, I feel it is time to become more financially comfortable and empower others with the opportunities I have created.

This is a land of wealth we travel upon so why settle for less. Being born in a place of poverty although there are much worse places than West Philly on 60th and Lansdowne, I have to continue to remove myself from a mentality of being Poor. Which I have heard the acronym **Passing Over Opportunities Reportedly**. Now it's time for me to get off this train and get prepared to do this music video for Oddboy Roy, which I am doing at a very fair price to accommodate him. It's my way of giving back by making the video affordable for the young brotha. I'll speak with you at the final entry tonight.

A New Beginning
11:11pm

Throughout the year when I couldn't sleep I wrote, when I felt I had something important to share to the world I wrote. In my mind I hear the great words of *Frank Sinatra*, " and now the end is near and I face the final curtain." I could go on to quote a lot of the lyrics but much more than this, **I did it my way.** My wife is asleep next to me on the couch and my daughter Wisdom is in her bedroom sleeping. The video shoot turned out great earlier and it was an honor to work with the youth to help them facilitate their dreams. I just submitted my trademark for the *Timeless Masterpiece logo* which feels like a great step in the right direction to take things to the next level. This chapter is over and I look forward to the future, within me I have movies, children books, a great visual documentary, and a host of other visions that will take time to manifest.

Final Thoughts

As cliché as it sounds, follow your dreams, nothing can stop you but you. Yes, life will be just that **"Life"** and if you have been paying attention there are no guarantees how it will play out. As long as you are conscious you have the ability to move forward. Never backwards only move forward, yes take the time to reflect on the past, but build on the foundation of which you know to be true. I know you have a desire within you or else we would not be able to relate. Keep the fire burning bright within you and with that fire shine to guide others to victory. There will be opposition, for no great victory can be won without.

Let the obstacles that come your way make you stronger and wiser. Don't fall victim to yourself, know your weaknesses, have knowledge of self as we like to say within the conscious world. If you are aware of the things that cause you to stumble along the way, consider us fools to continue to walk in the same ditch. If you are one of the few people in this world that feel problem free, please do your best to brighten the days of others for you never know how far your kindness will encourage someone else.

Be forgiving to those who deserve to be forgiven and keep in mind some people you have to keep at a distance because unfortunately they can drag you down and hold you back. It's hard to discern these moments at times but you have to weigh those relationships for yourself.

It takes time to be timeless...

I'm not aware of the time of year it is for you but for me this year is coming to a close as I write, regardless of the time period WE remain, I dedicated my life to be a champion, a hero, a representation of the light of God. My mission is to create and inspire, to provide light for the lost who hope to find themselves in a better place. As the clock winds down to midnight at 11:48pm I choose to wake up my wife to enjoy the end of the year with her and be the best husband and father I can be. She was disturbed by the sound of the typing and left the room but that was her choice. As I said before we can't force our loved ones to know the importance of our missions. Don't penalize them for not sharing your passion if you are blessed to have someone to build with, you don't have to have the same interest 24-7.

Let it be known I felt blessed to be a free thinker and have the courage to manifest thoughts in to reality. Life is truly enjoyable when you walk in faith and not in fear working towards achieving your goals. Be the best you can be and never stop growing. Find the necessary time to pause and enjoy the fruit of life within the process of your pursuit. Peace & Many Blessings... ENJOY LIFE

"Infitain" Sean Mitchell Caldwell

XII

AQUARIUS – I KNOW

WISE WORDS

HEARD FROM 107 DIFFERENT PEOPLE

1.JOE P.

DON'T LET YOUR EMOTIONS SUPERCEDED YOUR INTELLIGENCE.

2. BILL LINK

THE KEY TO KNOWLEDGE IS TO DOUBT...

3. GOLDO

THE GODDESS OF LUCK WILL ONLY BLESS THOSE WHO ARE PREPARED

4.TIM

WHEN ONE PERSON SAYS NO JUST KEEP GOING

5. LLOYD WILLIAMS

TREAT PEOPLE THE WAY YOU WANT TO BE TREATED

6. YOGA MAYI

PATIENCE & PERSEVERANCE ARE THE KEY TO SUCCESS IN LIFE.

7. STEVE NICOL

YOU CAN'T CHANGE THE WIND, BUT YOU CAN ADJUST THE SAILS AND GO WITH IT.

8. SUGE V

HATE & RACISM IS TAUGHT NOT INHERITED...

9. MITZI LONGMORE

.IMPOSSIBLE CAN MEAN I AM POSSIBLE IT DEPENDS ON YOUR PERSPECTIVE

10. SUSAN MANBARA

ROME WAS NOT BUILT IN ONE DAY. KEEP BUILDING

11. TOREY THORPE

EACH ONE TEACH ONE STEP UP AND REACH ONE

12. MERLIN WOLF

I DO NEED HELP FIXING MY WINGS BUT WHEN I FLY YOU WILL SEE.

13. NEAL

YOU HAVE TO KNOW WITHIN YOUR MIND AND WITHIN YOUR HEART THAT GOD IS ALWAYS WITH YOU.

14. SHARON BALL

RESPECT, PRIDE AND DIGINITY ENCOMPASED IN LOVE...

15. DJ SMALLS

STAY INSPIRED STAY MOTIVATED AND NEVER GET DISCOURGE.

16. ABDUR RAHMAN KANTAMANTO

TRUST BUT VERIFY

17. STEPHAN MEUNIER

DELAYED PROGRESSION IS BETTER THAN INSTANT SUCESS

18. CHRIS W

THE ANTICIPATION OF DEATH IS WORSE THAN DEATH ITS SELF

19. MCKERSIN

QUESTION EVERYTHING IN LIFE AND COME TO YOUR OWN CONCLUSIONS.

20. WILLIAM DAVIS

THE WISEST ADVICE I'VE HEARD IN MY LIFE IS TREAT PEOPLE THE WAY YOU WANT TO BE TREATED.

21. TOGA ROBERTS

NEVER PLAY NUMBER 2 IN A NUMBER 1 WORLD.

22. ERIC

IF YOU ARE GOING TO COMMIT YOURSELF TO SOMEONE BEING IN BUSINESS OR PERSONAL BE SURE THEY ACCEPT YOU FOR YOU.

23. ABDUL MAJID

KNOWELEDGE PROCEEDS SPEECH AND ACTION. THE MANIFESTION OF SOMETHING SEEN AND NOT HEARD.

24. VID

CHAPTERS END AND NEW ONES START ...YOUR LIFE IS A MOVIE...WRITE YOUR LIFE

25. ISA

THE FOUNDATION IS GOD, BUT THE MANIFESTION TO REVEAL ITSELF IS ALMOST IMPOSSIBLE,

26 RAHMAN RICHARDSON

ATTITUDE IS IMPORTANT, BUT IT IS GRATITUDE THAT BRINGS FORTH HAPPINESS...

27. TOMMY 84 YEARS OLD

YOU HAVE TO DO WHAT YOU WANT TO DO, LISTEN TO THAT LITTLE VOICE THAT GUIDES YOU.

28. STEVE LOOS RECLOOS

NEVER CHANGE YOUR ENERGY FOR ANYONE ELSE...

29. SEAN GRAHAM

DON'T TAKE NOBODIES CRAP...

30. MIKE VARGAS

ALWAYS KEEP LEARNING, KNOWLEDGE IS THE TOOL THAT YOU WILL NEED TO SUCCEED

31. TREE

STAY WITH GOD

32. BOB EUERLE

SPEAK WHAT YOU WANT, PRAY FOR WHAT YOU WANT, BUT DON'T EVER PRAY FOR WHAT YOU DON'T WANT THATS FOR DAMN SURE.

33. JULIAN TAVERAS L

BE CONSISTENT WITH WHAT EVER YOU DO

34. PHISH TODD SCHENCK

CAN WE LIVE WHILE WE ARE YOUNG?

35. CALVIN WILLIAMS

THE MARTIAL ARTIST GREATEST WEAPON IS TO BE ABLE TO DEFEAT HIS OPPONET WITHOUT USING HIS HAND OR FEET, BUT YET BY USING HIS MIND

36. UNKOWN

WE MESURE OUR STRENGTH BY THE STRENGTH OF OUR ENEMIES. THE BEST AND BRIGHTES OF US WILL NATURALLY RISE WITHIN SOCIETY.

37. RUSSELL ESPOSITO

SOMEBODY HAS TO BE A CONDUCTOR OF THIS SYMPHONY OF CHAOTIC MADNESS

38. SHOUKRY

TAKE YOUR TIME AND HURRY UP.

39. MR. TAYLOR

NEVER LET YOUR GUARD DOWN BECAUSE YOU WILL BE PREPARED FOR WHAT FOR COMES YOUR WAY

40. GARY OBRIAN

SOMETHINGS IN LIFE YOU DONT GET BROWNIE POINTS FOR. SOMETHINGS ARE WHAT THEY ARE

41. EARL BOYD

THE BEST WAY TO MAKE MONEY IS TO SOLVE A PROBLEM.

42. TED LEWIS

DONT GIVE UP... PEOPLE WILL TALK YOU OUT OF YOUR DREAMS.

43. RAM RICHES

WE ALL HAVE SOMETHING TO OFFER, WE ALL HAVE SOMETHING TO LOSE.

44. UNKOWN

AN OBSTACLE IS WHAT YOU SEE WHEN YOU TAKE YOUR EYES OFF THE GOAL

45. JOE V

WHEN YOU ARE AT YOUR WORST LOOK NEXT TO YOURSELF AND YOU WILL SEE SOMEONE WORST THAN YOURSELF... KEEP YOUR HEAD UP

46. CARMELO & TALASIA

PATIENCE IS KEY. GOOD THINGS COME TO THOSE WHO WAIT.

47. SUPREME

RECOGNIZE THE GOD ACTIVITY THAT CONNECTS US ALL WHICH IS LIFE

48. CHALAS

BETTER TO SERVE THAN TO BE SERVED

49. JEREMY NAPOLEON (REMY)

THE WORST ENEMY YOU HAVE IN YOUR MIND IS FEAR, DOUBT, AND WHEN YOU STOP DREAMING

50. SAID BAAGH

DONT FOLLOW OTHERS, BE YOURSELF

51. BORN

EVERYTHING PASSES, ITS A SEASON TO BE HAPPY AND A SEASON TO BE SAD.

52. MATTY C. (FINGER)

SERINITY PRAYER

53. JOHNIE WRIGHT

IF SOMEBODY OFFERS YOU SOMETHING TAKE IT BECAUSE IF THEY DIDN'T WANT YOU TO HAVE IT, THEY WOULDN'T HAVE OFFERED IT IN THE FIRST PLACE.

54. A. HAROLD DATZ, ESQ.

"POWER IS TO BE EXERCISED WITH HUMILITY & RESTRAINT."

55. ABULLAH RAHMAN

NEVER TAKE THE ELEVATOR TO GET TO THE TOP, ALWAYS TAKE THE STAIRS

56. P.B JR

THERE WAS ONCE A WISE MAN WHO BEGAN TO SPEAK THEN HE WAS NO LONGER CONSIDERED TO BE WISE

57. INF THE AUTHOR

CHARACTER IS FORMED THROUGH ADVERSITY NOT COMFORT

58. JEREMY GUERRA

IT'S WHAT'S REAL OVER WHAT YOU FEEL. FACTS OVER FICTION.

59. YEHUDAH

RESPECT OTHERS AS YOU WANT TO BE RESPECTED...

60. ALFRED FISHER

BELIEVE IN YOURSELF, EVEN WHEN IT SEEMS IMPOSSIBLE. KNOW "I CAN".

61. COACH RAY LILLEY

FIRST YOU SHOULD BE SELFISH, SO YOU CAN LEARN AND UNDERSTAND YOURSELF THEN BECOME SELFLESS TO BECOME MORE VALUABLE TO OTHERS.

62. DR. EDGAR CODD COURSTESY OF ALAN

ACCURACY CONSISTENCY; COMPLETENESS AND INTEGRITY

63. RONYA RICH

LOOK BOTH WAYS

64. ANDRE THE BOOKMAN

GOD IS MY BOSS, AND I WORK IN A WAREHOUSE AND EVERY HUMANBEAN IS A BOX AND GOD SAYS PICK UP THE BOX OFF THE GROUND AND PUT IT ON THE TOP SHELF.

65. RALPH OBRIEN

DON'T BE AFRAID TO TAKE A CHANCE.

66. ZEUS

QUITING WHILE YOUR AHEAD IS NOT THE SAME AS QUITING

67. ALEX WANDER

MINUTES FROM HER MASTERPIECE MINUTES TO MIDNIGHT.

68. YUSEF

NOTHING DESERVES WORSHIP, BUT ALLAH AND MUHAMMAD IS HIS MESSENGER

69. UNKOWN

WE NEED MORE FATHER FIGURES IN THIS WORLD

.

70. JOHN HILL

NEVER CHASE A MAN OFF A CLIFF

71. KRISTEN TULLI CALDWELL

IT DOESN'T MATTER WHAT'S IN YOUR HEART IT MATTERS WHAT'S DONE

72. MACINTOSH SMITH

WORDS HAVE MEANING, WORDS HAVE MASS, WORDS CARRY WEIGHT

73. DARBY CANEEN

WHEN YOU THINK YOU DID ENOUGH ALWAYS DO ONE MORE

74. JAMES DOWNING

RECOVERY IS NOT A DESTINATION ITS A JOURNEY

75. EDDIE MEAT

A SUCCESSFUL MAN ONCE SAID MY ONLY REGRET IN LIFE IS THAT I DIDN'T AIM HIGHER.

76. BERNIE TULLI

MEASURE TWICE CUT ONCE.

77. KATHY TULLI

HONESTY IS THE BEST POLLICY

78. TANK PLUMMER

SALITUDE HAS SOFT SILKY HANDS BUT WITH ITS STRONG FINGERS IT CAN CHOKE THE HEART TO ACHE.

79. CALVIN ANDERSON

SANICTAFATION IS A LIFE LONG JOURNEY BUT SALVATION IS INTENTION

80. DAVID GREGO

DON'T BELIEVE ANYBODY THAT SAYS THE WORD CAN'T.

81. QUINN SPENCE

THE BEST YEAR-ROUND TEMPERATURE IS A WARM HEART & A COOL HEAD.

82. ANTHONY ADAMS

THE FEAR THAT YOU FEEL IS NOT REAL

83. IBN QAYYIM COURTESY ABDUR RAHEEM

IT'S BETTER TO BE IN A SITUATION THAT REQUIRES PATIENTS THEN ONE DOES NOT.

84. RICH TIRRELL

ALIENS TOLD ME TO CHOOSE WHAT YOU WANT OUT OF LIFE AND DO IT

85. LULA HOSEY GRANDMOTHER KENNETH JACKSON

WHAT EVER YOU DO IN LIFE DON'T YOU EVER GIVE UP. NOT ONLY DO YOU GIVE UP ON YOURSELF YOU GIVE UP ON ME.

86. GEORGE SCIARRONE

WHEN YOU DON'T HAVE A PLAN, YOU PLAN TO FAIL

87. PETER ALLEN

THERE IS PLENTY OF ROOM IN THE UNIVERSE FOR GOD

88. AYANNA LOTT

AGING ISN'T OPTIONAL BUT GETTING OLD IS

89.. UNKOWN

IN ORDER FOR YOU TO SET YOUR GOALS AS HIGH AS YOU WANT THEM, YOU HAVE TO CHALLENGE YOURSELF TO ACCOMPLISH THEM.

90. MATTHEW FOX

IF SOME ONE IS SCARED YOU SHOULD NOT HARM THEM. DO ON TO OTHERS AS YOU WANT DONE TO YOU

91. RAYMOND H.

TOUGH TIMES DON'T LAST TOUGH PEOPLE DO

92. RON HARRIS

KNOWLEDGE, WISDOM, UNDERSTANDING AND TAKE CARE OF YOUR HEALTH

93.. JERRY GARCIA - KAREN ALLEN

LIFE MAY BE SWEETER FOR THIS I DONT KNOW FEELS LIKE IT MIGHT BE ALRIGHT

94. TANK

SOMETIMES TOO MUCH IS NOT ENOUGH...

95. DAVID CHAMBERS

SOMETIMES THE RIGHT THING IS NOT DOING THE RIGHT THING...

96. JONAH AMEDEO

I KNOW I AM EXACTLY WHERE I AM SUPPOSED TO BE.

97. NOBLE DREW ALI - ADAMS EL

WHEN ONE SALES FOR GAIN HEAR THE WHISPERING OF CONSCIOUSNESS AND DON'T TAKE ADVANTAGE OF THE BUYER

98. ISH

NOBODY DESERVES TO WIN BUT ITS PREPARATION AND HARD WORK WHAT DETERMINES THE VICTORY.

99. ALEXIS MITCHELL

I DON'T PUT ANYTHING PAST ANYONE, BECAUSE I DON'T PUT ANYTHING PAST MYSELF.

100. REYSH ALEF FRIDMAN

CREATING IS A HORIZON RATHER THAN A DESTINATION; A CALLING, NOT A CAREER.

101. SHAMBHU

.LISTEN TO YOURSELF, YOU ARE YOUR BEST TEACHER.

102. DAVID WILLIAMS

DON'T LET ANYBODY RUSH YOUR PROCESS

103. BIG WIL

DO THE BEST THAT YOU CAN DO AND UNDERSTAND YOU CAN'T HELP EVERYBODY.

104. EDOSÈ OMOWALÈ

RE-MEMBER YOUR-SELF...

105. ELVIN BURRISON

A SLOW NICKEL IS BETTER THAN A FAST DIME.

106. BROTHA REGGIE

MY STRENGTH LIES IN THE ABILITY TO CONTAIN MY EMOTIONS NOT THE ABILITY TO EXPRESS THEM

107. WALI HAKIM

WINNERS MAKE THINGS HAPPEN AND LOSERS LET THINGS HAPPEN.

"Infitain" Sean Mitchell Caldwell

WRITTEN BY
" INFITAIN " SEAN MITCHELL CALDWELL

ILLUSTRATED BY
ROB WOODS

TIME
TRAVELER

Written by Infitain
Illustrated by Rob Woods

Copyright ©2017

Can't stay stuck in the past, keep it moving,

Time will pass you by fast keep it moving.

How many hours do you got

BEFORE THE HAND OF TIME STOP...

AS I ROSE FROM tHE WatERS BaPtIZED In tHE ESSEnCE

A Man tHat DOn't WORK DOn't Eat MY FIRSt LESSOn

LOOKED UP anD WaS amaZED, MOtIVatED BY tHE SUn

GOt a tHOUSanD MILES aHEaD OF ME tOOK OnE StEP

JOURnEY BEGUn

GUIDED BY a HUNGER tHat NEEDED tO BE SUPPRESSED

anD OnLY GOt MY InstInCts nOtHInG MORE nOtHInG LESS

BROKE a BRanCH OFF a tREE tURnED It IntO a StaFF

GOT THE FEELING I'M BEING FOLLOWED,

HOPING THE FEELING WOULDN'T LAST

SEEING THE SHADOWS BELOW, THE VULTURES ABOVE ME

FLYING

aWaitinG MY DEatH MY FIRSt EnCOUntER WitH a LION

LOOKED DEEP In HIS EYES anD It LOOKED BaCK IntO MInES

It's LIKED WE LOOKED FaMILIaR BUt It WaS OnE OF OUR

tIMES.

THE LION LEAPED (BAD MOVE) READY TO RIP ME APART.

BUT I WAS SHARP STOOD MY GUARD AND PIERCED HIM RIGHT

THROUGH HIS HEART

FROM tHE BUSHES COMES tHE FIRSt WOMAN PLAYING HER

PARt BROUGHt ME FRUIt JEWELS AND VEGEtABLES tHE KING

HAS MADE HIS MARK (TIME TRAVELER)

Can't stay stuck in the past, KEEP it MOVING,

TIME WILL PASS YOU BY FAST KEEP It MOVING.

HOW many HOURS DO YOU GOt

BEFORE tHE HanD OF tIME StOP...

Sitting upon my throne in a land known as Kemet

Surrounded by diamonds being worshiped

by royal subjects

A Nubian God clothed in the finest garments

It's a statue being built of me at this very moment

72 Harlots can't fulfill my lust corrupted by power

In this kingdom what's considered yours, is ours

What's mines is mines kept my people in bondage

Don't respect nothing not even my Goddess

SHE TELLING ME I LOST MYSELF AND THAT I NEED TO BE

HUMBLED CURSED MY NAME AND LEGACY

TO SEE MY EMPIRE CRUMBLE MY FATHER WAS THE OPPOSITE

HE WAS JUST FAIR AND HONEST

I THOUGHT HE WAS WEAK AND LIVED LIFE TOO MODEST

HE DIED OF OLD AGE AND NOW THAT I'M THE PHARAOH

IGNORED ALL HIS LESSONS AND MADE MY EXIT FROM HIS

SHADOW, I PROPOSE A TOAST TO THE MOST IMPORTANT

PERSON TOOK A DRINK FROM MY CHALICE THEN

I'M KILLED BY THE POISON

(TIME TRAVELER)

Can't stay stuck in the past, KEEP It MOVING,

TIME WILL pass you BY Fast KEEP It MOVING.

How many HOURS DO YOU GOt

BEFORE tHE HanD OF tIME StOP...

1921 GREENWOOD TULSA OKLAHOMA OWNED A BUSINESS

WITH LAND RECEIVED A COLLEGE DIPLOMA

3 BEAUTIFUL CHILDREN A WIFE THAT COMPLIMENTS ME

WAS ALL I CAN BE PROUD TO SERVE MY COUNTRY

Ignorant times exist but here Moors are living just

Fine Unified and Strong Blessed with a peace of mind

We circulate our money built our own economy

Hospitals and banks thank you O.W Gurley

WHEN HE FIRST ARRIVED AND PURCHASED 40 ACRES

ENTERPRISE ON THE LAND AND NEVER ASKED FOR FAVORS

A TRUE MAN OF FAITH SOWED AND THEN HE REAPED

THEY CALLED US LITTLE AFRICA...BLACK WALL STREET

It's May 31st LEAVING WORK AND I'M TIRED

HEARD ABOUT 50 GUNSHOTS THAT HAD TO BE FIRED

SCREAMING CHILDREN BURNING BUILDINGS

DESTROYED BY HATE

APPROACHED BY A MAN

WEARING A WHITE PILLOW CASE THEN....

"Infitain" Sean Mitchell Caldwell

XIV

TARUS – I HAVE

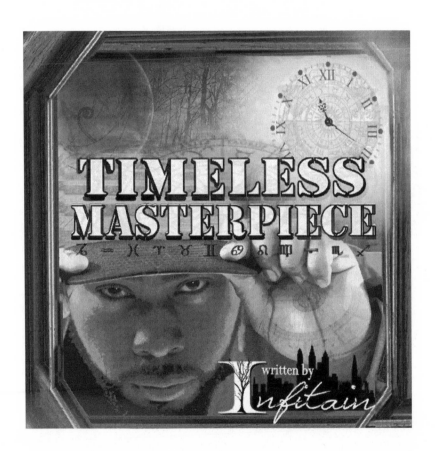

ALBUM LYRICS

Timeless Masterpiece (Aries)

Finger to the sky one-time thanking God,
because I came from nothing just a right state of mind
every day I was hustling, you seen the sold-out signs
CDs and DVDs scrolling through your timeline.
Riding through the city watching Wisdom in the mirror
the future's looking bright I couldn't see it any clear,
taking care of business, I'm about to disappear - on my
way to an island 7 miles in the air. Masterminding my
next move reclined in the chair, got my head in the
clouds and it's hard to see you there, unless you already
here as we proceed the gain velocity giving back to the
poor creating jobs providing salaries.
Making wise decisions, prepared for rainy days, save
spend invest in intellectual properties.
Working hard stack that 401k or incorporated the
business and formed an LLC.
Shoebox filled with money bank account on a bean,
got the safe locked with bonds, gold and jewelry.
Donations made to the 501c3 making sure every year we
file that Schedule C.
Plant your vegetables in May, if you're anything like me.
That seed you sowed was old still getting fruit from the
tree.
Cup over flowed watching everybody eat, now I'm
thinking generations and I practice what I preach. Hold
Up....

Pennies for my thoughts 16 bars and some hooks,
playing chess not checkers just castled with the rook.
The king is in position, squared if you listen, kept a
conscious vision

plans to get it with good intentions.

No government checks just hard work and persistence
plans to stay connected I don't speak too much to
bishops.

Wise counsel from the nights mainly my queen calls me
Sean,

Strategically moving forward seeing value in pawns.

I'm like cut the check, I'm an entrepreneur a Hilltop
Hustla West Philly in this jawn.

Paying homage to the soil, represent 24 from the day I
was born until the second I hit the floor.

Now it's International Inf still walking with the limp. the
bol 4444real the Kyser Soze of this -

I was more than just a rapper, it was more than just a
name, it was more than just a label it was never about the
fame.

See I never like to stunt I prefer to be humble, you can
build something up and you can watch as a crumble and
that's facts from a man that built something from
nothing.

Set some goals and get the trapping then it's on to the
next one

and if you can't relate to nothing I'm feeling sorry for
you.

But if you recognize the truth then we on the same
pursuit.

Don't matter if you're struggling or tailored in a 3-piece
suit.

Inshallah we make it happen regardless what we do.
TIMELESS…

I Know What It's Like (Taurus)

I know what it's like to have to do for self,
Going against the odds with the cards you were dealt
Father incarcerated, Mother with diminishing health,
Watching her pass away feeling like you ain't got
nothing else.
I know what it's like to get up and follow your dreams,
keeping the faith regardless of how hard it seems.
Visions of tomorrow looking better than yesterday,
A walking inspiration feeling the pressure every day.
Making history, call it destiny
focus on a goal making moves like its meant for me
Sometimes I can't explain it but work ethic is the recipe,
Watch your thoughts manifest in the physical
Now that's a necessity,
I Know What It's Like

Smiley Face (Gemini)

I'm thinking back to my darkest hour, no food no gas no
electric, no power
Man when it rains it pours showers and I was all alone,
rent overdue and it was time to move on.
Just a Momma's boy suffering, lost her to cancer it was
devastating crushing,
And I was just Sean, no INFITAINMENT, no husting,
But that all had to change it was either drown in my
sorrow or rise and do my thing.
Vividly struggling, working 3 jobs just to survive I was
juggling.
Thoughts in my mind I had to quit, bugging,
Because I knew that I was more, started up a label now
I'm an entrepreneur
And it wasn't easy, it was hard work
Trials and tribulations all the lessons I learned
Try to play it cool but inside you feel broke
Sometimes life is so demanding you got to fight through
it all
walk by faith and keep on standing.

(2x)
And I always felt it inside of me, through the struggle
through the pain,
I just kept pushing and believe, that one day, I still would
make a smiley face…

I was just two years old when my father went to prison
and I'm from the hood good chance I be there with him.
But I ain't no statistic success is what I envisioned,

Young bol out there pitching out there playing his
position.
Did 28 years came home criminal minded
Show him it's a better way but the streets they had him
blinded
Regardless that's my Pop the mirror keeps me reminded
Rebellious blood in my veins Most High keep grounded
Because I'm grinding and it's easy to get caught up
Temptation around me grateful for my portion and that's
enough
but kept on climbing because its higher heights to reach
already made a quarter million legally in these streets.
so, if worse comes to worse we still winning
climb from the bottom then went back again
came back from 0 so many times started stacking them
We built our own doors nobody let us in.

(2x)
And I always felt it inside of me, through the struggle
through the pain,
I just kept pushing and believe, that one day, I still would
make a smiley face…
Now I'm a father my daughter watching these lyrics.
Teach her right from wrong Knowledge of God in her
Spirit
Say it Loud wit understanding so she can feel it
ABC's 123's and a Metaphysics
Speaking success into existence as we persist through
resistance
Turn our visions to missions
Sharing with scholars who listen

Spend more time doing then wishing think before making decisions
Representing the definition of ambition
Standing with power so that the world see
The time is ours making it first mentally
Write your own books tell your own history
We need more than just players it's time to own the league
Now as we proceed I know it's hard to believe
How we made it this far without the bread or the cheese
From eating syrup sandwiches to gourmet meals from overseas
I saw the impossible was possible at least that's what I perceived.

(2x)
And I always felt it inside of me, through the struggle through the pain,
I just kept pushing and believe, that one day, I still would make a smiley face...

Time Traveler (Leo)

Can't stay stuck in the past, keep it moving,

Time will pass you by fast, keep it moving.
How many hours do you got
Before the hand of time stop…
(2x)

Guided by a hunger that needed to be suppressed
and only got my instincts nothing more nothing less
Broke a branch off a tree turned it into a staff
Got the feeling I'm being followed, hoping the feeling
wouldn't last.
Seeing the shadows below, the vultures above me flying
awaiting my death my first encounter with a lion
Looked deep in his eyes and it looked back into mines
It's liked we looked familiar, but it was one of our times.
The Lion Leaped (bad move) ready to rip me apart.
But I was sharp stood my guard and pierced him right
through his heart
From the bushes comes the first woman playing her part
Brought me fruit jewels and vegetables the king has
made his mark
(TIME TRAVELER)

Can't stay stuck in the past, keep it moving,
Time will pass you by fast keep it moving.
How many hours do you got
Before the hand of time stop...
(2x)
Sitting upon my throne in a land known as Kemet

Surrounded by diamonds being worshiped by royal
subjects
A Nubian God clothed in the finest garments
It's a statue being built of me at this very moment
72 Harlots can't fulfill my lust corrupted by power
In this kingdom what's considered yours, is ours
What's mines is mines kept my people in bondage
Don't respect nothing not even my Goddess
She telling me I lost myself and that I need to be
humbled
Cursed my name and legacy to see my empire crumble
My father was the opposite he was just fair and honest
I Thought he was weak and lived life too modest
He died of old age and now that I'm the Pharaoh
Ignored all his lessons and made my exit from his
shadow
I propose a toast to the most Important person
Took a drink from my Chalice then I'm killed by the
Poison
(Time Traveler)

Can't stay stuck in the past, keep it moving,
Time will pass you by fast keep it moving.
How many hours do you got
Before the hand of time stop…
(2x)

1921 Greenwood Tulsa Oklahoma
Owned a business with land received a college diploma
3 beautiful children a wife that compliments me
Was all I can be proud to serve my country.
Ignorant times exist but here Moors are living just fine
Unified and Strong ... Blessed with a peace of mind
We circulate our money built our own economy
Hospitals and banks thank you O.W Gurley
When he first arrived and purchased 40 Acres
Enterprise on the land and never asked for favors
A true man of faith sowed and then he reaped
They called us little Africa...Black Wall Street
It's May 31st leaving work and I'm tired
Heard about 50 gunshots that had to be fired
Screaming children burning buildings destroyed by hate
Approached by a man wearing a white pillow case
then....

Best Life Possible (Libra)

Grown, can't do things that kids do
Bad choices brought me back what to I been through.
Wise words got me through all the obstacles
Focused to live the best life possible
Working doing better than I ever been
Better credit new car switched my residence blessed and
Grateful for the evidence and everything I aint got is
irrelevant
A wise Man told me Health is Wealth
So handle the business taking care of yourself
What's a couple dollars with no plans.
The past was a present in time we got use it
took a minute stayed committed made a mark
More than just a label deeper than the charts
With this art, I got to play my part
Live the best life possible and the mind body spirit sharp

Live the best life possible

I know addicts and atheist that walk with God
Religious folks blinded engulfed in facades.
People with plenty money not happy with their lives
and people that's poor that rise because they tried.
A Singer with a voice that worked harder than me
A Legend in the game made a name up in the streets.
Showed the whole world seen him on TV
But committed suicide because his pain was to deep
We all feel the weight sometime life can be heavy
Keep a conscious state of mind stay active and healthy
What's knowledge if not applied drinking water like
Wisdom

Got to think healing before acknowledging symptoms
Who am I but you but with a different perspective
Only moving forward it's all about progression
I see you over I'm headed in the same direction
Live the best life possible information the best medicine

Shine the Light (Libra)

Struggle Addiction Lost Pain Poverty Shame Broke
Trapped feeling like we can't Maintain

But I'm a shine the light
You gonna shine the light
They gonna shine the light
We gonna shine the light

Death Anger Lost Faith Hate Mistakes the fake but the
real can relate

New York shine the Light
Jersey shine the light
Chicago shine the light
Philly shine the Light

Life is what you make it regardless of inception
Half full Half empty it's based on your perception.
There's a blessing in a lesson
learn and keep on pressing
When life gives you lemons....
Bag them up and sell them
It's a gift in the present while you planning for the future
learning from the past Sankofa ...Hakuna Matata
No Worries that's why I'm rarely in a hurry Building with
my brethren
speaking life to my shorty
Got a Daughter name Wisdom
Don't feel like I'm pushing Forty
Gray hairs in my beard head filled with war stories
1 time for the glory prayed and found a way out

A hood that was vicious some took different route
It's an Ol head shining that know what I'm talking about
Owned their house for years
Worked hard raised their kids
And I was there
Blessed when I left my apartment
Dedicated - to the light shining in the darkness

Struggle addiction lost pain poverty shame
Broke trapped feeling like we can't maintain

But I'm a shine the light
You gonna shine the light
They gonna shine the light
We gonna shine the light

Death Anger Lost Faith Hate Mistakes the fake but the
real can relate

Detroit shine Light
Atlanta shine the Light
Ohio shine the Light
Cali shine the Light

Same story different book
Can't recite the verse but memorized the hook
You know the song it's the journey not destination
Turn a negative circumstance to a winning situation
Grind over vacation
Major moves take patience
Workaholic or focused just concrete
no roses

Shine the Light to give the truth more exposure
Listening to the Most High that's walking right beside us
I'm not talking about religion I'm speaking metaphysical
The science of faith that can get you through what's
difficult
Some call it a miracle some don't acknowledge the
spiritual
Guess that's to be determined by the
Walk of the individual
Can't say I would have made it
without looking to something greater
Couldn't do it myself so acknowledged the creator...
Now my life is good
still praying regardless
Dedicated to the light that's shining in the darkness

Struggle Addiction Lost Pain Poverty Shame Broke
Trapped feeling like we can't maintain

But I'm a shine the light
You gonna shine the light
They gonna shine the light
We gonna shine the light

Death Anger Lost Faith Hate Mistakes the fake but the
real can relate

Europe shine the light
Haiti shine the light
Jamaica shine the light
Africa shine the light

With the good come the bad
With the light comes darkness
If aint nobody sick, It's no need for the doctor's office
There's guidance in silence finding answers inside us
A little l Kemetic science Maat for the balance.
Was a product of my environment now excuses is useless
Don't know life can't know death Confucius
Only the wisest and the stupid never change
and I ain't the same still stepping up my game
and I ain't trying to be vain or worried about fame
Just heard when I was young that I could accomplish
anything
Still living by the statement
Started INFITAINMENT
Dreamed - Believed - Worked Hard- Achieved It
Never forgot where I came from
and all I had to go through
The experience was priceless and now I understand the
value.
Building up you building up me Oneness
Dedicated to the light that's shining in the darkness...

Philly Memoirs (Cancer)

It's the Bol Infitain going to share some Philly Memories.
6-0 Hilltop it was never a mystery.
Broad and Chestnut I know they missing me.
But I'm out New York, infiltrating the industry.
I been on my grind before I the new millennium
Flipping Abe, Alex, and Drew, converting them in to
Benjamins
Most my singles went to Chinese, and Dominicans
But the hood get my dividends
And this was just the beginning, soon as I lost my mom I
lost my mind.
Friends wasn't too far too high to witness me fall
Josh and Pooh was there probably recall it all
Juice was in college while I lost everything, thank God I
had a dream
It was INFITAINMENT more than just a label sitting
with A&A, Logic and Brent at the table.
Now Authentic a teacher and Al stay in the booth and
Brent, went on to make beats for the Roots.
Me and B, started hustling, going down South street and
grinding these albums.
That's word to Maj the subway profit,
Ask Apple Martini being broke not an option.
Spoken Word drop the caged bird cypher it was nobody
like her 1 time for Xavier.
Tomahawk put out hustle or starve.
Magnum O had the science and mathematics in their bars
Los moving mixtapes off the skateboard
And Joe Noise was a beast when I heard him on the
guitar.
I seen a lot on my journey to the top

I was the streets watching while I was posted on the
block.
Jafar Barron on the horn, Urban drumming Shamans on
the strip.
Mighty Mouse exclusive bussing back flips.
Henry David Bernardo wrote it in the Black Star
K.P, Just Greg at the Pearl of Africa.
Fiya Chick Air It Out, Black and Nobel
Feya and Blu, put me on that Rotunda
Exodus bill.
And before the Superstar I knew D R as Feek
Shouts out to West Philly 6-0 Dell P
Corey Wims, Eskay, Power Team bombing things,
Kasino, MilliBless. Merk City, Swat Team,
I was in weed cyphers with O.G and Reed Dollaz, the
chronic gone but the memories Timeless.
A Thousand barz from NH at the Hut
Before Mista Heard got with freeze and birthed DAUS.
Before Nitty drop the Roscoe, before Iniko came home.
I Know Brasco from AMarriage entertainment.
Shouts out to Butch Amun and Cliff Montana,
A couple of hustlers I recognized when I came up.
I was at the 5 spot when Vodka and Chic Raw was there
And that's when. My vision became more clear
We made it!
VIP with Young Chris, studio sessions with Brom.
Shaking hands with Beanie Sigel, Questlove showed me
love bussed it up with Black Thought
Charlie Baltimore, Peedi Crakk and Neef Buck.
Shouts out to Joey Jihad and Chill Moody, Machete
King, Sage Listen, and Prime City.
Dozi did my first beat we called it Trumpin. Sold over
50,000 units to keep my name buzzing. Philly History!

Wisdom (Scorpio)

Best thing that ever happened to me,
my Daughter I dedicate this to you
We named you Wisdom because your words have power
Spoke that into your life before you seen your first hour.
I prayed for you, stayed for you, examined my world.
Became a better man for you.
I'm your father and I say that with pride, grew up around
some homes where the word dad didn't reside.
Knew I made a decision that would change my life
But I'm the type of Man that always focus on the light at
the end of the tunnel
regardless if it's dark no matter where you walk keep love
in your heart
and that's the secret and I pass that on to you, you was
born a queen but you got to stay true.
For yourself, your fam, and especially the Most High, no
matter where you are peace and love will reside
Wisdom…

Rule number 1 is respect and
with that it ain't no other rules left.
Always for yourself and everybody you come across
Even if they lost confused and when you know they
wrong.
A soft answer turns away wrath. You don't always have
to prove your point but instead
Remain humble but never be gullible Look people in
their eyes you can see through their soul.
Watch Out for lust don't confuse that with love.
Don't settle for less and always do your best, persistence
beats resistance and you can have anything you want

because you attract what you think about and that's the secret I pass this on to you,
You were born a Queen, but you got to stay true, for yourself your fam, and especially the Most High. No matter where you are peace and love will reside...
Wisdom

Miracles (Capricorn)

Born in the struggle destined to make it
as I reach for the stars seeing my name encrusted on
I did it for the ghetto with ambition in my soul, so I rose
up out the hood and took it to another level
Gotta own something stay consistent hope you listening
Persistence beats resistance hashtag winning is the
mission
Follow I know sometimes our options seem shallow.
It's either hustle or starve but that's a hard pill to swallow.
Never gonna quit never gonna stop, climbed from the
block on our way to the top We gonna make it
It's no debating with myself or somebody hating I'm
going to continue embracing thing grind and practice
patience.
Pops doing bids over 20 years still there.
Lost my momma and face my biggest fears and shed
tears and I'm still here.
Still standing I'm the man when I look in the mirror this
is all that I'm hearing.

(2x)
I'm never gonna quit, never gonna stop, climbed from the
bottom on my way to the top you are looking at a
miracle, something comparable, never gonna quit never
gonna stop straight to the top.

Often, I woke up just to grind, remembering times when I
didn't have a dime
I had to get my seen the future then I climbed
A dream became a plan success the definition
Knowing that I'm the one I stepped up out the Matrix.

Self-employed 10 years it was a test but still I faced it.
You can say I aced it, failed when it came to hating
too busy with my brush and I'm focused on what I'm
painting and I'm still stroking.
Speaking to the storms in any ocean putting my faith in
motion.
Doing me and my options open,
you better be specific what you speak into existence it
can happen in an instance reference Music over Business.
The first of many flipping pennies to Benny's but blew it
on henny, sipping old e end and blazing plenty.
The glamorous life but some beg to differ in that Cool C
flow.
That's for my Philly representors.

(2x)
I'm never gonna quit, never gonna stop, climbed from the
bottom on my way to the top you looking at a miracle,
something comparable, never gonna quit never gonna
stop straight to the top.

Sometimes I doubt if I can though
finding myself back where I came from then I look back
army foundation I'm here
Still building I'm focused overdue shut off notices, no
food for the mice or the roaches, Broke!
That's why I was on the grind all the time getting my
cake up early in the morning probably before you even
wake up.
Still I rise you can see it in my eyes working hard to
enterprise
INFITAINMENT more than just a label

I know I'm able watching out for Cain and the Judas at
my table
Miracles, transcending from the spiritual manifest in the
physical, I bring it to you lyrical.
One in the same, changing the game building my name,
you heard of me it's the bol Infitain,
Don't know? Well you can google or ask about me, on
my job 4444real entrepreneur making deals.

(2x)
I'm never gonna quit, never gonna stop, climbed from the
bottom on my way to the top you looking at a miracle,
something comparable, never gonna quit never gonna
stop straight to the top.

Sleepless Knights (Sagittarius)

Lion on the Prowl plotting looking for the sheep,
Pen versus paper scrolls covered with the ink
Building with the army sleepless knights heavyweight
Infitain, Nicoritti, Cappaccino the great,
Cyphers with the clan paying homage to the Wu
They say that Philly dirtball cleaned up nice
Came a long way from three wings and the rice
Now it's something exotic anytime that I like,
Break bread with the poor to curb their appetite
Food for thought always watch with the third
Circulate that dollar stack a portion what you earned
Never bounce a check that you wrote with your word
And he who grinds always get what they deserve.

Let It Go (Aquarius)

Few things stay the same the seasons always change
Looking back and now I see the difference
Lives change from decisions in an instant
Got a Vision then you got to go and get it
First job I ever had was on Lansdowne Ave
West Philly 6-0 making cash Cleaning toilets Mopping
floors
I was a gopher, go for go for that those days are over
Back then all I wanted was to rock Sean John
1999 and I wasn't online No facebook you couldn't do it
for the Vine
Comfortable in Myspace before Tom
Fast forward to the future I was working 3 jobs at the
same time
Infitain was always on his grind
Then I realized
I could work this hard for me
Clocked in and Sold Out
Now the rest is history. I Let it Go

Chorus

Now I'm on to the next
Miss me when I'm gone busy looking for the best
Knight in shining armor but that wasn't how I dressed
Came through with my hoodie on she wasn't impressed
Trying to stay afloat swimming 7 days a week
Got my good enough she got a college degree
Late phones calls when she couldn't get no sleep
Subliminal Messages….

Now my paper wasn't always right to go and make that
move
I was dealt a different hand wore different pair of shoes
Should've known how it is you wasn't born with silver
spoons
and you know what they say about Time healing wounds
Woke up and smelled the turkey bacon, burnt pancakes
filled with cinnamon and raisins
Strolled through memory lane picked a Tulip from a
garden
It was fun while it lasted but now I think it's time we let
it go

(Be Free). You got the freedom to Win
The freedom to lose the freedom of choice the freedom to
choose. Weigh your options if yours go and get it
have a plan stay consistent and persistent
Don't listen to the haters and doubters that you come
across.
Take advice from the wise when you lost.
The truth is in the stars keep your head to the sky.
Sometimes you can't be high if you really trying fly
and sometimes the truth hurts if you realize it's a lie
It's like you at the top and they telling you, you can't
climb
Take a look at where you came from and far you about to
go
staring back at the reflection at the person you used to
know
Changed for the better still get reminded of your past
You had to get low to build the momentum if they ask
It's not about who's fast it's about what you endure
On your mark get set get ready, now let it go...

Glad that We Did It (Pisces)

If I could start from scratch do the same thing twice
Quit my job again make it harder for my life.
Valuable lessons through the struggle paid the price
Flip something out of nothing moving units day and night
All I did was just get up and grind,
it's easy to get lost along the way sometimes
Keep moving forward go and follow the signs
Be about your business stay focused and shine
Woke up in the morning then I pointed to the sky
Even when it's cloudy you got to see the silver line
Glass half full optimistic state of mind
Salute to the soldiers in the struggle 1 time
Going to sleep late still the first to awake
Early bird with the worm putting food on the plate
If you working harder than the rest, then Sean can relate
Because I ain't never wanted to be nothing in life but
great.

So glad that we did it...

"Infitain" Sean Mitchell Caldwell

ABOUT THE AUTHOR

"Infitain" Sean Mitchell Caldwell was born and raised in West Philadelphia November 7th, 1983. His father Woodrow Mitchell found himself sentenced and incarcerated to 30 years in prison while Infitain was at the age of 2 years old. His Mother Linda Caldwell did her best to raise him and his older brother Terrell within a community where they could easily find themselves influenced negatively. This book documents an entire year of the Author as he worked towards manifesting his elaborate creative vision known as Timeless Masterpiece. Revealing the past, present and future.

TimelessMasterpiece.com

Made in the USA
Columbia, SC
21 September 2022

67355343R00107